SCOTT M. FRALEY

Social Media Marketing Secrets

The Ultimate Guide to Boosting Engagement, Elevating Your Brand, Driving Sales, and Growing Your Business Across All Major Platforms

This book was professionally typeset on Reedsy.
Find out more at reedsy.com

Contents

Introduction   1

Chapter 1: Understanding the Social Media Landscape   4

   1.1 Overview of Popular Social Media Platforms   5

   1.2 Platform Popularity and Usage Statistics   8

   1.3 The Role of Myth Busting   11

   1.4 Unique Features of Each Platform   15

   1.5 Understanding Audience Demographics   17

   1.6 Final Thoughts   20

Chapter 2: Crafting Compelling Content   22

   2.1 Content Types That Drive Engagement   23

   2.2 Storytelling Techniques for Brand Building   25

   2.3 Visual Content Creation Tips   29

   2.4 Enhancing Authenticity and Trust   31

   2.5 Maximizing Engagement through In-
   novative Strategies   34

   2.6 Final Thoughts   37

Chapter 3: Building a Robust Brand Presence   38

   3.1 Developing a Consistent Brand Voice   39

   3.2 Creating Brand Guidelines   41

   3.3 Cultivating an Authentic Online Persona   44

   3.4 Leveraging User-Generated Content   46

   3.5 Training Your Team   48

   3.6 Final Thoughts   52

Chapter 4: Driving Engagement Through Interaction   54

4.1 Implementing Effective Call-to-Actions (CTAs)   55

4.2 Engaging with Comments and Messages   58

4.3 Hosting Live Events and Q&A Sessions   61

4.4 Using Feedback for Content Creation   63

4.5 Building Community through Interaction   65

4.6 Final Thoughts   68

Chapter 5: Converting Followers into Customers   70

5.1 Creating Compelling Lead Magnets   71

5.2 Crafting Compelling Offers   74

5.3 Designing Targeted Ad Campaigns   78

5.4 Utilizing Retargeting Strategies   81

5.5 Monitoring and Improving Campaign Performance   84

5.6 Final Thoughts   86

Chapter 6: Leveraging Influencer Partnerships   88

6.1 Identifying the Right Influencers for Your Brand   89

6.2 Negotiating Influencer Agreements   92

6.3 Measuring the Impact of Influencer Marketing   95

6.4 Understanding Niche Influence   98

6.5 Engagement Beyond Numbers   100

6.6 Final Thoughts   103

Chapter 7: Harnessing Analytics for Success   104

7.1 Key Performance Indicators (KPIs) in Social Media   105

7.2 Interpreting Social Media Metrics   108

7.3 Adjusting Strategy Based on Data Insights   111

7.4 Implementing Analytics Tools   114

7.5 Maximizing Engagement Through Data   117

7.6 Final Thoughts   119

Chapter 8: Exploring Advanced Marketing Techniques   121

8.1 SEO Strategies for Social Media 122

8.2 Integrating Email Marketing with Social Media 125

8.3 Innovative Content Distribution Channels 128

8.4 Cross-Promotion Techniques 131

8.5 Analytics and Optimization 134

8.6 Final Thoughts 137

Chapter 9: Staying Ahead of Social Media Trends 139

9.1 Identifying Emerging Social Media Trends 140

9.2 Experimenting with New Features 143

9.3 Adapting to Platform Algorithm Changes 147

9.4 Participating in Industry Communities 150

9.5 Analyzing Competitor Strategies 152

9.6 Final Thoughts 156

Chapter 10: Case Studies and Real-World Applications 157

10.1 Successful Brand Campaigns Analysis 158

10.2 Lessons Learned from Failures 161

10.3 Adapting Case Study Strategies to
Your Business 163

10.4 Leveraging Emotional Connections in Branding 165

10.5 The Role of Community Engagement
in Marketing Success 168

10.6 Final Thoughts 171

Chapter 11: Overcoming Common Challenges 173

11.1 Dealing with Negative Feedback 174

11.2 Managing Social Media Crises 176

11.3 Preventing Burnout in Social Media Management 178

11.4 Establishing Effective Communication Protocols 182

11.5 Promoting Positive Engagement and
Brand Loyalty 184

11.6 Final Thoughts   187

Chapter 12: Resources for Continuous Learning   188

   12.1 Accessing Industry-Leading Tools
and Platforms   189

   12.2 Subscribing to Credible Newsletters
and Podcasts   192

   12.3 Engaging with Community Forums
and Networks   195

   12.4 Leveraging Educational Resources for
Skill Development   197

   12.5 Monitoring Industry Trends and Innovations   201

   12.6 Final Thoughts   204

Conclusion   205

References   209

Introduction

Social media has transformed the way businesses communicate and engage with their audiences. For many entrepreneurs and business owners, navigating this vast digital landscape can seem daunting. You've likely found yourself buried under endless information about social media marketing, trying to discern which strategies are most beneficial for your business. The struggle is real, and it's shared by countless others who feel immobilized by the enormity of this task. But imagine a scenario where you not only understand the social media world but also harness its power effectively. This book is designed to be your guide in achieving precisely that.

Today's business environment demands an active social media presence. Consumers increasingly rely on social platforms for recommendations and insights into products and services. As an entrepreneur, staying aloof from social media isn't just an oversight; it's a missed opportunity. With 73% of marketers affirming that their social media efforts have been effective, the potential benefits cannot be overstated. Social media impacts brand visibility, customer engagement, and ultimately, sales. It's essential to recognize and embrace this shift if you wish to remain competitive in today's market.

I vividly recall the instant my Instagram post took off and went viral. It wasn't simply the influx of likes that caught my attention. What truly captured me was the stream of comments and messages pouring in from followers eager to learn more about what I had to offer. That single incident triggered a passion within me to delve deeper into social media marketing. From that moment forward, I understood how crucial these platforms were for connecting with and understanding my audience. My journey wasn't just about mastering algorithms or creating visually appealing posts; it was about building genuine relationships and cultivating a community around my brand.

Now, you might wonder: What exactly will you gain from this book? Rest assured, this book provides more than just theories and concepts; it's packed with actionable strategies, real-world case studies, and expert advice designed to give you a competitive edge. You'll discover how to craft content that resonates with your audience and develop a deeper under-standing of platform-specific nuances. Whether it's engaging in meaningful conversations or turning casual followers into loyal customers, the insights presented here aim to equip you with versatile tools for success.

By embarking on this reading journey, prepare yourself for practical exercises that encourage hands-on learning. Each chapter will introduce new strategies tailored to your unique needs while offering analytical perspectives on industry trends. As you progress, you'll feel empowered to take decisive actions that drive your business forward. Our goal is to provide a pathway for you to elevate your brand using tested and proven methods – all while staying attuned to shifts in consumer behavior and technological advancements.

Let's face it: Success in social media isn't about chasing every trend or flooding feeds with content. It requires a thoughtful approach driven by creativity, consistency, and clarity of purpose. Through structured guidance and insightful examples, this book champions a balanced strategy that aligns with long-term business goals. We'll explore how to measure effectiveness, pivot strategies when needed, and leverage the ever-evolving features and formats of different social media platforms.

Ultimately, this book aspires to bolster your confidence and competence in managing social media endeavors, regardless of the scale of your operation. Whether you're a startup aiming to create buzz or a seasoned business professional seeking to re-fine your tactics, the knowledge shared here is applicable across different industries and demographics. Prepare to rethink how you connect with audiences, enhance brand recognition, and drive growth through strategic social media engagement. Let us embark together on this transformative journey into the vibrant world of social media marketing.

Chapter 1: Understanding the Social Media Landscape

U nderstanding the social media landscape is essential for anyone wanting to build a strong online presence today. In this digital era, social media platforms have become incredibly influential in shaping how people communicate and interact. They offer unique opportunities for entrepreneurs, marketers, and social media managers to engage with audiences at multiple levels. By tapping into these digital tools strategically, individuals and businesses can enhance their visibility, connect more deeply with consumers, and ultimately drive business achievements. Whether aiming to increase brand awareness or seeking new ways to reach potential customers, knowing the intricacies of various social media channels is pivotal.

The chapter delves into the mechanics of major social media platforms and the distinctive advantages each provides. From Facebook's vast user base and advertising capabilities to Instagram's visual storytelling strengths, each platform offers something different. Twitter, or X, allows for real-time interaction, while LinkedIn serves as a hub for professional networking and B2B marketing. TikTok stands out for its creative video content and ability to go viral among younger demographics. This chapter will guide readers through understanding these platforms' features, revealing how they operate and what makes them effective for particular audiences. It will also highlight the importance of identifying where a target audience is most active and how trends on these platforms can inform a dynamic marketing strategy. By exploring these elements, readers will gain a comprehensive view of how to navigate social media effectively, ensuring that their strategies align with both current platform practices and anticipated future shifts in digital engagement.

1.1 Overview of Popular Social Media Platforms

Navigating the social media landscape is crucial for entrepreneurs, marketing professionals, and social media managers aiming to successfully establish their brand presence. In today's digital age, understanding the nuances of major platforms is key to executing effective marketing strategies that lead to increased engagement and sales.

To start, let's explore some of the key social media platforms commonly used in marketing efforts: Facebook, Instagram, Twitter (now known as X), LinkedIn, and TikTok. Each of these platforms serves a distinct purpose and caters to different types of audiences.

Facebook remains one of the most powerful tools for marketers due to its extensive user base. Known for being a platform where brands can establish meaningful connections with consumers, Facebook's versatility allows businesses to share content in various formats—text, images, and videos—catering to a wide range of demographics. Its advanced advertising options, like targeted ads, enable companies to reach specific audience segments based on interests and behaviors, thus maximizing marketing impact.

Instagram, largely visual-based, is an ideal platform for brands looking to engage with younger audiences, particularly Millennials and Gen Z. The platform's emphasis on aesthetics can be leveraged through visually appealing images and stories. Instagram's interactive features such as polls, quizzes, and stories are excellent for driving customer engagement and gathering insights into customer preferences.

Twitter, or X, provides a unique environment for brands to join real-time conversations. It's an advantageous platform for sharing quick updates, news, and engaging directly with customers through replies and mentions. Twitter's character limit encourages concise communication, which can help distill marketing messages efficiently and promote viral campaigns.

LinkedIn stands out as the go-to platform for B2B marketing, professional networking, and thought leadership. With its focus on industry professionals, LinkedIn provides businesses an opportunity to connect with decision-makers and influencers within their field. Companies using LinkedIn effectively often post expert content, job opportunities, and industry insights that foster community engagement and enhance brand authority.

TikTok has gained significant traction among younger generations, especially Gen Z. Known for its short-form, creative video content, TikTok presents an innovative approach to brand storytelling and authenticity. Marketers can take advantage of trends and challenges to boost content visibility and engagement. The platform's algorithm favors creative expression and interaction, making it a fertile ground for viral marketing campaigns.

Recognizing where your target demographics are most active is pivotal to optimizing marketing efforts. For instance, demographic data shows that Snapchat is favored by 18-29-year-olds, while Instagram appeals to both 18-29 and 30-39 age groups. Meanwhile, LinkedIn is popular among those aged 30-49, catering to professionals seeking business-oriented content. Understanding these dynamics helps in channeling resources to platforms with the highest potential for reaching desired audiences and achieving marketing objectives.

For a strategy to remain effective, it must be adaptive to the prevailing trends on each platform. Trends act as valuable indicators of what captivates current audiences, allowing businesses to tailor their content strategies accordingly. As social media evolves rapidly, a tactic successful today might lose relevance tomorrow, necessitating constant refreshing based on the latest trends and data points.

Trending content on Facebook often includes live videos and interactive posts, while Instagram sees high engagement with behind-the-scenes content and user-generated materials. On Twitter, hashtags drive trend participation, enabling brands to align with popular topics and expand reach, whereas LinkedIn trends center around professional development topics and industry news. TikTok trends lean heavily on creativity and entertainment, favoring brands that can skillfully integrate themselves into viral movements.

Staying ahead requires marketers to consistently monitor platform-specific trends, demographic changes, and algorithm updates. This vigilance ensures strategies remain aligned with audience expectations and technological advancements, preventing outdated tactics from undermining marketing success.

1.2 Platform Popularity and Usage Statistics

In today's digital age, the social media landscape is an ever-evolving arena where understanding user engagement is paramount. This knowledge not only helps in crafting effective marketing strategies but also provides insights into how audiences interact with various platforms. User engagement statistics offer valuable data on how different platforms cater to distinct audiences. Platforms like Facebook, Instagram, and Snapchat have fundamentally unique audience bases that influence marketing decisions significantly.

Facebook, for instance, boasts a diverse demographic range, attracting users of nearly all ages. Marketers harness this diversity by tailoring content that appeals to broad segments, from teenagers to older adults. In contrast, Instagram predominantly attracts younger audiences, often between 18 to 29 years old, which influences brands to create visually appealing and trend-driven content to capture their attention. TikTok's explosive growth exemplifies catering specifically to Gen Z, leveraging short-form video content that prioritizes entertainment and creativity. This distinction allows marketers to plan platform-specific campaigns that resonate most effectively with target demographics.

Similarly, trends in platform growth can inform future engagement strategies. The rise of TikTok has been a key development, with its rapid increase in monthly active users—showing a significant preference among younger audiences for short, engaging video content. Such trends guide marketers toward developing dynamic visual content strategies tailored for TikTok or similar emerging platforms. Meanwhile, professional networking site LinkedIn continues to grow amongst professionals aged 25 and above, suggesting that B2B marketers need to focus more on thought leadership content and industry-specific discussions.

Furthermore, keeping abreast with emerging data trends plays a crucial role in maintaining a competitive edge. Social media algorithms are continuously updating, shaping how and when content reaches audiences. Being informed about these changes enables marketers to optimize their timing, format, and type of content they publish, ensuring maximum visibility and engagement. For instance, the increasing emphasis on video content across platforms suggests businesses should invest more in video production capabilities.

Moreover, evolving privacy regulations globally affect user engagement methodologies. Understanding these regulations helps businesses adapt their data collection strategies accordingly, fostering trust while still gaining valuable consumer insights. Such adaptations may involve shifting from third-party data dependency towards first-party data collection, enhancing direct interactions with consumers through personalized experiences.

As new features emerge—such as ephemeral content and live broadcasting—they offer novel opportunities for engagement, demanding that businesses remain agile and ready to integrate innovative tactics into their strategy. Recognizing and swiftly adopting these features ensure brands stay ahead in capturing user interest.

To capitalize on these insights, businesses should regularly review updated statistics and reports from credible sources. Leveraging tools like Google Analytics or platform-specific analytics dashboards can provide actionable insights into audience behaviors and preferences. This real-time data enables enterprises to make informed decisions quickly, adjusting their approach based on what resonates with their audience at any given time.

Additionally, collaboration across departments within an organization can foster a comprehensive understanding of user engagement. Marketing teams, along with sales and customer service, can share valuable user feedback and behavioral insights. This cross-functional approach ensures marketing strategies align cohesively with broader business objectives, leading to more personalized and effective customer engagement tactics.

For entrepreneurs and small business owners aiming to establish their brand presence, understanding these statistics helps in identifying the right platforms and the most effective types of content for their target audience. Small businesses can leverage niche markets by analyzing competitor engagement and benchmarking their performance against industry standards.

Marketing professionals benefit from integrating these data insights into strategic planning. By setting measurable goals based on platform-specific engagement rates, they can refine campaign tactics to optimize performance. Moreover, continuous learning through webinars, workshops, and industry conferences keeps them updated with the latest trends and techniques in social media engagement.

Social media managers, tasked with executing these strategies, should prioritize staying current with platform updates and best practices. Regular training sessions and network engagements with peers allow them to exchange ideas and discover new ways to improve engagement metrics.

1.3 The Role of Myth Busting

In the complex and ever-evolving world of social media, myths often emerge, leading businesses astray. Addressing these misconceptions is crucial for maximizing the potential of social media marketing and avoiding common pitfalls.

One of the most pervasive myths is the belief that a presence on every social media platform is necessary for success. This misconception can lead to the inefficient use of resources.

Rather than spreading efforts thinly across multiple platforms, businesses should focus on where their target audience is most active. Each platform has its unique strengths, user demographics, and engagement patterns, allowing businesses to tailor their strategies accordingly. For instance, Instagram's visual-centric approach may be perfect for fashion brands, while LinkedIn provides an ideal environment for B2B services.

Dispelling the myth of platform ubiquity opens up opportunities to explore lesser-known channels that might offer untapped potential. Emerging networks like Threads or newer entrants into the market often cater to niche audiences, which could align well with certain business objectives. By exploring these underutilized avenues, companies can find new ways to engage with audiences in meaningful, innovative ways.

Another common fallacy is the idea that social media marketing only serves the top of the sales funnel, focusing solely on building awareness and interest. Social media's true power lies in its ability to drive engagement through all stages of the customer journey. Platforms like Facebook and Twitter enable businesses to build strong relationships by interacting directly with their audience, thus facilitating not just initial interest, but also conversion and retention. Creating compelling content and engaging in conversations helps establish trust and authority, encouraging potential customers to transition through the sales funnel effectively.

Moreover, believing that viral content is the holy grail of social media success is another trap. While virality can significantly boost visibility, it is often unpredictable and driven more by luck than strategy. Instead, businesses should focus on creating consistent, high-quality content that resonates with their specific audience. This approach results in more sustainable growth and engagement, fostering stronger community ties. Investing time in understanding what truly captivates one's audience ensures that content remains relevant and shareable, regardless of whether it reaches viral status.

Additionally, the demographic misconception, which assumes social media caters exclusively to younger audiences, can limit a brand's potential reach. Although platforms like TikTok are popular among younger users, social media, in general, hosts a diverse range of age groups. Platforms such as Facebook and LinkedIn have significant adult user bases, making them invaluable for targeting older demographics. Recognizing this diversity allows businesses to tailor their messaging to suit the preferences of different generations, thereby broadening their market reach.

The myth surrounding artificial intelligence (AI) replacing marketing roles is another cause for concern among industry professionals. However, AI should be embraced as a tool for enhancement rather than a threat to jobs. AI can efficiently manage tasks like scheduling, posting, data analysis, and even crafting personalized messages, freeing up marketers to focus on strategic planning and creative execution. By leveraging AI to support campaigns, marketers can achieve greater efficiency and effectiveness, ultimately enhancing their impact in the digital space.

To dismantle these and other myths, businesses must adopt a

mindset of continuous learning and adaptation. As new trends and technologies emerge, staying informed about changes in consumer behavior and platform capabilities is critical. Regularly reviewing analytics and performance metrics helps refine strategies, ensuring they are aligned with current market conditions.

For those venturing into social media marketing, understanding the importance of tailoring marketing strategies for each platform's audience is essential. A single unified strategy rarely fits all; successful campaigns require customization to match the nuances of each channel. Developing a clear understanding of how audiences interact on various platforms allows businesses to craft messages that resonate clearly and persuasively.

Creating audience personas is also an invaluable tool in shaping effective social media strategies. Businesses can better target their marketing efforts by developing detailed profiles that include interests, behaviors, and preferences. These personas provide insight into the types of content that will engage and convert users, guiding marketers in developing content strategies that truly speak to their intended audience.

Ultimately, dispelling myths about social media platforms equips marketers, entrepreneurs, and businesses with the knowledge needed to navigate this landscape successfully. By leveraging accurate information and data-driven insights, they can avoid common pitfalls and capitalize on the myriad opportunities that social media offers. The key to thriving in this dynamic environment lies in being willing to question assumptions, remain flexible, and continually adapt strategies to align with shifting trends and consumer expectations.

1.4 Unique Features of Each Platform

In understanding the social media landscape, it's essential to recognize the distinct features and functionalities that set each platform apart. This knowledge allows businesses and marketers to leverage these platforms effectively for brand growth and customer engagement.

A key aspect of social media is the news feed algorithms used by major platforms like Facebook and Instagram. These algorithms are designed to optimize content visibility, ensuring that users see what they are most interested in. They prioritize content based on user interactions, such as likes, comments, shares, and even time spent on posts. For entrepreneurs, small business owners, and marketing professionals, understanding these mechanisms can significantly impact content strategy effectiveness. By aligning content creation with algorithmic preferences—like incorporating eye-catching visuals or engaging narratives—businesses can enhance their visibility and reach within target audiences. It's about crafting content that resonates and encourages interaction, thereby boosting its chances of being promoted in users' feeds.

Another standout feature of social media is temporary content, such as Instagram Stories and Facebook Live. These formats offer unique opportunities for real-time engagement, a crucial element in today's fast-paced digital world. Instagram Stories, for example, allows businesses to connect with their audience through ephemeral content that disappears after 24 hours. This feature adds a layer of urgency and exclusivity, encouraging quick viewer response and fostering a sense of connection through authentic, behind-the-scenes glimpses or timely updates. Similarly, Facebook Live offers a dynamic platform for direct interaction with followers, from live Q&A sessions to product demonstrations. It bridges the gap between brands and consumers, creating an interactive dialogue that builds community and trust.

Moreover, the integration of e-commerce functionalities across various social media platforms has transformed them into powerful sales channels. Platforms like Instagram and Facebook have incorporated shopping features that allow businesses to tag products directly in posts or stories, leading customers seamlessly to purchase pages. This development streamlines the shopping process, making it easier for consumers to discover and buy products without leaving the app. For marketers and business owners, this means not only increased sales potential but also the ability to track consumer behavior and preferences more accurately through integrated analytics. Whether it's leveraging Instagram's shoppable posts or Facebook's marketplace, these tools enable brands to reach consumers at multiple touchpoints, enhancing overall shopping experiences and driving conversions.

Each platform's unique capabilities present different advantages for maximizing brand presence and engagement. For instance, Instagram's visual-centric format favors businesses with strong imagery, offering creative avenues for storytelling through photo and video. Meanwhile, Facebook's extensive data insights provide granular targeting options that help refine audience segmentation and personalize marketing efforts. These tailored approaches enhance message relevance and increase engagement rates, ultimately contributing to strategic brand-building initiatives.

For those managing social media, keeping abreast of ongoing changes and emerging trends is vital. Platforms continually update their features and algorithms, making adaptability a cornerstone of effective social media strategy. By staying informed and agile, businesses can better anticipate shifts in the social media ecosystem and adjust their tactics accordingly, maintaining competitive advantage in a rapidly evolving digital environment.

1.5 Understanding Audience Demographics

Understanding audience demographics is crucial for anyone looking to establish a robust presence on social media, whether they are entrepreneurs, marketers, or social media managers. A key component of this understanding is the breakdown of demographic profiles by platform, which serves as a foundation for creating targeted content that resonates with specific consumer groups.

Different social media platforms attract distinct audiences based on factors like age, gender, location, and occupation. Facebook, for instance, tends to have an older user base compared to Instagram, which is more popular among younger users. LinkedIn is predominantly used by professionals seeking networking and career opportunities, while TikTok has rapidly gained popularity among Gen Z. Recognizing these demographic differences allows businesses to tailor their messages appropriately. For example, a brand targeting young millennials may prefer Instagram's visual-centric approach, using eye-catching imagery and interactive stories to engage this demographic effectively.

Moreover, insights into psychographics and user behavior further enhance the ability to create content that truly resonates with the audience. Psychographics go beyond basic demographics by delving into the psychological characteristics of consumers, such as their values, beliefs, and lifestyles. Understanding these elements helps in developing marketing strategies that align with the emotional and cognitive triggers of the audience. For instance, if a business knows that its target audience values sustainability, it can emphasize eco-friendly practices and products in its campaigns to foster stronger connections and engagement.

Analyzing psychographic data also provides valuable insights into user behavior. By observing patterns in how people interact with content across different platforms, marketers can identify what types of posts generate the most engagement. This might include examining the times of day when users are most active, the kinds of content they share, or the sentiments they express through comments and reactions. With this knowledge, businesses can adjust their publishing schedules and content types to better meet the expectations and preferences of their audience.

As social media continues to evolve, so do the demographics of its users. Therefore, it's essential for businesses to keep abreast of these changes and adapt their marketing strategies accordingly. For example, as younger generations begin moving toward new emerging platforms, marketers must pivot their focus to maintain relevance and capture the attention of these potential customers. Similarly, shifts in societal norms and cultural trends can influence user behavior and preferences, necessitating periodic reevaluation of marketing approaches to ensure alignment with current values and attitudes.

Evolving demographics also demand a dynamic understanding of audience segmentation. Instead of relying solely on static data, such as age or income, businesses need to continuously monitor how demographic groups are changing over time. This could involve analyzing how life events, such as graduating from college, starting a family, or switching careers, impact consumer needs and behaviors. By staying informed about these developments, businesses can proactively adjust their messaging and offerings to remain relevant to their target audience.

Additionally, leveraging technology tools can significantly aid in the collection and analysis of demographic and psychographic data. Platforms like Google Analytics and social media insights tools provide detailed reports on audience characteristics and behavior patterns. These insights empower marketers to test and refine their strategies with precision, allowing them to focus their efforts where they will have the greatest impact.

Ultimately, a comprehensive understanding of both demographic and psychographic profiles enables businesses to craft marketing messages that not only reach but also resonate with their intended audience. The integration of this knowledge into social media strategies ensures content relevancy, enhances customer engagement, and ultimately drives conversions and sales.

By viewing audience demographics as a living entity rather than a static dataset, entrepreneurs, marketers, and social media managers can gain a competitive edge. They become capable of predicting market trends, making informed decisions, and crafting personalized experiences that speak directly to the desires and motivations of their audience. As the social media landscape continues to shift, those who embrace this holistic approach to understanding their audience demographics will find themselves better equipped to leverage the full potential of social media marketing.

1.6 Final Thoughts

This chapter has explored the essential features and demographics of major social media platforms like Facebook, Instagram, Twitter (X), LinkedIn, and TikTok. Understanding these nuances helps entrepreneurs, marketers, and social media managers to tailor their strategies for brand growth and customer engagement effectively. Each platform offers unique opportunities based on its user base and functionalities. By recognizing where target audiences are most active, businesses can focus their efforts on creating relevant content that resonates with specific demographics. This targeted approach maximizes the impact of marketing campaigns and enhances audience connection.

It is vital for professionals managing social media strategies to adapt continuously to trends, algorithm updates, and demographic shifts. Staying informed ensures that tactics remain aligned with current consumer expectations and technological advancements. Emphasizing adaptable strategies allows brands to maintain relevance in the dynamic digital landscape while fostering meaningful interactions and achieving marketing objectives. Applying these insights will assist in crafting social media initiatives that not only reach a wide audience but also generate lasting engagement and drive success.

Chapter 2: Crafting Compelling Content

C rafting compelling content is essential for businesses aiming to capture and hold the attention of their audience in today's digital landscape. The ability to produce content that not only engages but also resonates with readers determines the effectiveness of any marketing strategy. Entrepreneurs, small business owners, and marketing professionals must prioritize understanding what makes content dynamic and relatable to maximize its impact. As consumers become more discerning, the demand for content that speaks directly to their interests and needs grows, making it crucial for creators to develop tailored strategies. Social media managers play a pivotal role in executing these strategies, ensuring that content aligns with the brand's goals while appealing to its target market. Leveraging various content types to foster interaction and build relationships is key to sustaining customer engagement.

In this chapter, diverse strategies for creating engaging content are explored, offering insights into how different formats can enhance audience connection and drive marketing success. Readers will learn about the significance of interactive posts and how these can facilitate two-way communication between brands and consumers. The chapter delves into the benefits of behind-the-scenes content, which helps in humanizing brands and building trust with followers. Additionally, the importance of user-generated content (UGC) is highlighted, showcasing how it can amplify brand credibility. Video content, being one of the most consumed media forms today, is examined for its potential in storytelling and capturing audience attention. Through understanding the preferences and behaviors of their target audience, business owners and marketers can refine their approaches, integrating these methods into their content plans. This section provides practical examples and actionable advice, equipping readers with the tools needed to elevate their content creation efforts and meet their marketing objectives.

2.1 Content Types That Drive Engagement

Creating content that genuinely resonates with audiences is an integral part of successful marketing strategies. This section explores various types of content that effectively engage audiences, addressing the importance of dynamic content.

Interactive posts hold a special place in content strategies due to their ability to encourage audience participation and foster deeper engagement. By creating content that prompts responses or actions from users, businesses can establish two-way communication which is key to building relationships. Examples include polls, quizzes, or surveys that invite audiences to share opinions or preferences, thus giving brands valuable insights into consumer behavior. Incorporating interactive elements not only increases user involvement but also helps personalize experiences, making the audience feel more valued and understood by the brand.

Behind-the-scenes content offers a unique opportunity for brands to humanize themselves, building trust and authenticity in the process. By sharing glimpses of everyday operations, team interactions, or product development, companies can showcase the real people behind the brand, fostering genuine connections with their audience. This type of transparency can be powerful, as it allows customers to see beyond the façade of a corporate identity to the authentic stories and values that define a company. Whether it's through casual photos, video snippets, or even live streams, showcasing the human side of a business can significantly enhance brand loyalty and create a sense of community and belonging among followers.

User-generated content (UGC) is another effective strategy that can amplify credibility and boost organic reach. Encouraging your audience to create and share content related to your products or services not only increases engagement but also exponentially expands your brand's visibility across different networks. UGC showcases real-life usage and satisfaction, providing authentic testimonials that other potential customers may find more trustworthy than traditional advertising. By reposting or engaging with user-generated material, businesses demonstrate appreciation for their customers while simultaneously encouraging others to join the discussion.

Video content has become paramount in capturing attention and allowing dynamic storytelling. It's no secret that videos are one of the most consumed forms of media, appealing to diverse audience preferences and facilitating better retention of information. Through visual narratives, brands can convey complex messages in an entertaining and digestible format, often leading to higher engagement rates. Explainer videos, short clips, and even live sessions provide opportunities for brands to connect with their audience on a deeper level, offering personalization and immediacy that static content cannot match. Platforms like YouTube and social media thrive on video content, making it an essential component of any modern content strategy.

To leverage these types of content effectively, it's crucial to understand the preferences and behaviors of your target audience. Entrepreneurs and small business owners should prioritize building strong relationships by integrating these methods into their content plans. Meanwhile, marketing professionals and social media managers can use these tactics to refine their digital strategies, ensuring alignment with current trends and preferences.

2.2 Storytelling Techniques for Brand Building

In today's fast-paced digital landscape, storytelling has emerged as a crucial tool for brands aiming to build strong connections with their audiences. By embracing narratives that highlight the mission, vision, and values of a company, brands can craft compelling content that resonates with customers beyond mere transactional interactions.

At the heart of effective brand storytelling is the cultivation of a compelling brand narrative. This involves weaving together a story that encapsulates the essence of what your brand stands for. When you clearly define and communicate your mission, vision, and values through storytelling, you engage your audience on a deeper level. For instance, consider a sustainable fashion brand whose narrative emphasizes its commitment to environmental preservation. By telling a story about how their clothing production reduces waste and uses eco-friendly materials, the brand not only communicates its core values but also appeals to consumers who share those concerns.

Moreover, character-driven stories can elevate your brand message by creating relatable characters that evoke empathy and connection. When audiences see themselves reflected in a story, they are more likely to engage with it emotionally. Take, for example, a fitness brand that shares the personal journey of one of its users overcoming health challenges to achieve a healthier lifestyle. By focusing on this individual's struggles and triumphs, the brand not only humanizes its offering but also inspires others facing similar situations.

In addition to character engagement, presenting conflict and resolution within brand stories adds drama and highlights problem-solving abilities. These elements draw audiences in, keeping them invested in the outcome. A tech company might illustrate how its software helped a struggling small business turn around its operations, detailing the challenges faced and the eventual success achieved through using its product. This narrative approach reinforces the brand's value proposition and underscores its role in overcoming obstacles.

Customer testimonials and success stories serve as powerful tools to provide authenticity to a brand's narrative. By sharing real experiences and tangible benefits from actual users, brands can establish credibility and trust. Imagine a skincare brand that features stories from satisfied customers who have experienced transformative results. These testimonials validate the brand's claims and foster trust among potential consumers who relate to the shared experiences.

An excellent illustration of storytelling's power is seen in Patagonia, an outdoor apparel company. Patagonia's narrative revolves around its commitment to environmentalism and adventure. By sharing stories of its founder's passion for climbing and the company's dedication to sustainability, the brand connects with environmentally conscious consumers. This devotion to meaningful storytelling not only solidifies Patagonia's identity but also fosters loyalty among its audience who identify with these values.

Another compelling example is Warby Parker, which revolutionized the eyeglass industry by making quality eyewear affordable and accessible. The brand shares its origin story about one of its founders losing his glasses and being unable to replace them due to cost. This narrative strikes a chord with anyone who has faced similar dilemmas and showcases the brand's solution-oriented approach, further enhanced by its Buy a Pair, Give a Pair program.

Airbnb also excels in utilizing storytelling by positioning its customers as the main characters in its brand narrative. By sharing user stories about unique travel experiences made possible through Airbnb stays, the brand creates emotional connections that transcend traditional accommodation services. These stories emphasize community, cultural exchange, and the personal touch of local hosts, thereby painting Airbnb as more than just a service provider.

Effectively incorporating storytelling into your brand strategy requires a thorough understanding of your audience. It's critical to recognize what your customers value and how your brand aligns with those values. Storytelling should aim to create positive emotional associations with your brand, encouraging empathy and fostering memorable experiences. By consistently sharing narratives across various platforms—from social media to websites—you can build a cohesive brand image that resonates with your target market.

To get started with crafting your brand's narrative, begin by clarifying your brand's mission and values. Ask yourself: What does our brand stand for, and how can we convey this through storytelling? Integrate these values into every aspect of your narrative, ensuring that each character, conflict, and resolution reflects them accurately. Next, gather stories from employees, customers, or even the history of your brand. These can serve as rich sources of material for your storytelling efforts.

Once you have developed your narrative, it is essential to share it effectively. Incorporate storytelling into your marketing materials, whether through website content, video campaigns, or social media posts. By continuously engaging your audience with narratives that resonate, you help cement your brand in the minds of consumers, differentiating it from competitors.

2.3 Visual Content Creation Tips

In the digital age, where attention spans are dwindling and visual content reigns supreme, crafting visually appealing content is an imperative strategy for capturing and holding the interest of your audience. To this end, the use of high-quality imagery is paramount. Professional-grade photos and videos not only establish a sense of credibility and professionalism but also serve as the initial hook in a visually-driven online landscape. Whether you're showcasing products, services, or brand stories, using sharp, vibrant images ensures that your content stands out and draws in viewers.

Moreover, maintaining consistency through a well-planned color palette can significantly enhance your brand's recognition and coherence across various platforms. A consistent color scheme helps create a distinctive brand persona, making it easier for audiences to identify and resonate with your content. For instance, brands like Coca-Cola and Tiffany & Co. have successfully used their signature colors—red and robin's-egg blue respectively—to foster an instant connection with their audience. When planning your social media strategy, consider incorporating two or three primary colors that align with your brand's identity. This approach not only creates aesthetic appeal but also ensures that your brand leaves a lasting impression.

When it comes to conveying complex information succinctly, infographics are invaluable tools. They transform intricate data into engaging and easily digestible visuals, enhancing both understanding and engagement. By simplifying information through charts, graphs, and illustrations, infographics elevate the ability of viewers to grasp and retain concepts quickly. Industries ranging from finance to healthcare utilize infographics to distill complex statistics into more manageable formats, which can lead to higher engagement rates as audiences are more likely to share these informative assets. Integrating infographics into your marketing strategy can position your brand as an authority on specific topics, thereby boosting your credibility and reach.

Beyond static images, leveraging multimedia elements such as videos and animations can significantly enrich storytelling. Videos are particularly effective tools for narrative expression, allowing brands to delve deeper into stories while engaging multiple senses. With audiences spending considerable time on platforms like YouTube, integrating video content becomes an essential facet of any successful content strategy. Animations and dynamic visuals not only captivate audiences but can also improve retention rates and boost visibility due to favorable algorithm dynamics. In particular, B2B marketers, acknowledging the draw videos have, plan to increase their investments in video content marketing, highlighting its growing importance in the contemporary marketing landscape.

To effectively harness the power of videos, select eye-catching thumbnails that entice viewers to click and watch. A carefully curated thumbnail acts as the first impression of your video content. Platforms like YouTube take note of the number of clicks a thumbnail receives, underscoring the importance of selecting images that promise value and intrigue. In addition, developing unique illustrations and animations tailored to your brand story adds depth and dimension, providing a rich layer of engagement beyond what static visuals can achieve.

Incorporating these visual strategies requires consideration of branding consistency and platform optimization. It's crucial to optimize your content for each platform's specifications to ensure it is presented in the best possible light. For instance, Instagram prioritizes high-resolution square images, while Facebook favors horizontal images. Optimization extends to sizing, file formats, and even captions to maximize audience reach and interaction. Illustrations, when used thoughtfully, should complement rather than overshadow other visual elements, ensuring a balanced and varied content feed.

2.4 Enhancing Authenticity and Trust

In today's digital landscape, the authenticity and trustworthiness of a brand are more crucial than ever. The choices brands make in content creation can significantly influence how they are perceived by their audience, shaping the level of trust that consumers place in them. One effective way to build authenticity is by offering behind-the-scenes content that provides transparency and a glimpse into the inner workings of a business. This approach humanizes the brand, allowing followers to feel included and fostering a sense of belonging. By showcasing day-to-day operations, team dynamics, or even the challenges faced, brands can create an environment where consumers feel part of the journey.

Behind-the-scenes content offers an unfiltered look into the brand's world, which many consumers find appealing as it breaks the barrier between the company and its audience. For example, sharing insights about product development processes or candid moments from team meetings can reveal the genuine efforts that go into creating a product, thereby enhancing consumer trust. Take Patagonia, for instance; the outdoor apparel company frequently shares updates on their environmental commitments and the work culture in their offices, reinforcing their authenticity and dedication to sustainability.

Another impactful strategy is leveraging user-generated content (UGC). UGC consists of photos, videos, reviews, and other forms of content created by consumers, offering a diverse range of perspectives and experiences. When users share content about a brand, it not only broadens the brand's narrative but also fosters a community spirit. Customers often perceive UGC as more authentic than traditional advertising because it comes from real people who have experienced the brand firsthand. A study cited in our research shows that 74% of European consumers find UGC more trustworthy than curated promotional content.

Brands like Starbucks have successfully integrated UGC into their strategies through campaigns like the #RedCupContest, encouraging customers to share creative photos with their branded cups. Such initiatives not only provide fresh content but also engage the community, making participants feel valued and heard. Furthermore, user-generated testimonials and reviews convey authentic customer satisfaction, influencing potential buyers' decisions and reinforcing the brand's credibility.

Crafting narratives focused on overcoming challenges is another powerful technique to establish a memorable brand identity. Stories that highlight resilience and problem-solving resonate with audiences on a deeper emotional level. These narratives demonstrate the brand's ability to navigate obstacles, reflecting its values and commitment to improvement. Sharing stories of past hurdles and the lessons learned from them can position a brand as reliable and robust, especially in times of adversity.

Brands can draw inspiration from renowned companies such as Apple, which has crafted compelling narratives around innovation and overcoming technological limitations. By focusing on their journey toward creating groundbreaking products, Apple has cemented its image as a pioneer in the tech industry. Narratives like these not only captivate the audience but also reinforce the brand's mission and core values.

Consistency in visual styles further contributes to building trust. A uniform visual identity across all platforms helps establish brand recognition and reinforces reliability. Consistent imagery, color schemes, and design elements can make a brand appear more professional and cohesive, instilling confidence in consumers. Visual consistency creates familiarity, and when consumers see similar aesthetics and messaging across different channels, it reassures them of the brand's stability and integrity.

Think about Coca-Cola's unwavering use of its iconic red color and classic logo. These elements convey a timeless brand image and evoke a sense of nostalgia and dependability. Maintaining such visual continuity in marketing materials and social media posts ensures that consumers instantly recognize and associate positive attributes with the brand.

2.5 Maximizing Engagement through Innovative Strategies

To devise innovative strategies that maximize audience engagement and amplify brand presence, incorporating interactive elements like polls and quizzes is a fundamental approach. These tools serve as practical methods for gathering immediate feedback and insights concerning consumer preferences. By integrating these elements into your content strategy, you enable an interactive dialogue with your audience rather than one-sided communication. This direct interaction allows businesses to gauge the interests and needs of their customers more accurately. For example, a clothing retailer might use a poll to ask which new style customers prefer, gaining valuable insights into customer tastes while simultaneously encouraging user participation.

Moreover, in-depth quizzes that challenge the knowledge or preferences of your audience can create engaging experiences that prompt users to converse about your brand, thus amplifying word-of-mouth marketing. Quizzes can also act as lead magnets by requesting user information like email addresses in exchange for personalized results, making them not only engaging but also effective tools for lead generation. In this way, quizzes and polls help maintain ongoing engagement while aligning your offerings to meet the changing preferences of your audience.

Another significant strategy involves crafting relatable, character-driven stories to evoke emotions and foster deeper empathetic connections with audiences. Stories that tap into human experiences tend to resonate more effectively because they engage the audience on a personal level, forming emotional bonds that traditional marketing messages might miss. Consider crafting narratives around characters that reflect typical customer personas, highlighting their challenges and triumphs. These stories can serve as powerful testimonials that showcase real-life applications and benefits of your products or services.

By leveraging storytelling techniques, you can guide your audience through a journey that humanizes your brand, ultimately fostering loyalty. Such narratives can be illustrated through blog posts, video content, or social media campaigns, offering versatile ways to connect emotionally with different segments of your market. The emotional resonance of well-told stories increases viewer retention and solidifies brand identity, encouraging consumers to trust and relate to your brand more deeply.

In addition to interactive content and storytelling, infographics and videos constitute shareable assets that expand your reach and facilitate knowledge dissemination. Infographics are particularly effective when complex data needs to be presented understandably and engagingly. They break down intricate information into visually appealing formats, helping audiences grasp key concepts quickly. As an education tool, infographics increase the likelihood that viewers will share them within their networks, thereby extending your content's reach beyond its initial audience.

Similarly, videos offer a compelling platform to capture attention and boost engagement. With the increasing consumption of video content across platforms, it's essential to prioritize this medium to stay visible and relevant. Videos allow dynamic storytelling, where concepts can be demonstrated interactively rather than just explained. Whether through tutorials, behind-the-scenes footage, or customer testimonials, videos can communicate intricate ideas concisely while engaging viewers emotionally. The versatility of video content makes it ideal for diverse platforms, each offering unique algorithmic advantages that further enhance visibility.

Utilizing video content also aligns naturally with platform-specific priorities, given the preference many algorithms have for video over static content. Social media platforms like Instagram, Facebook, and TikTok often favor video posts, providing them with greater reach and engagement rates. By investing in quality video content, brands can ensure they remain front and center in their audience's feed, meeting algorithm demands while catering to viewer preferences for rich multimedia experiences.

To maximize the effectiveness of these strategies, it's crucial to approach content creation as an integrated effort rather than isolated tactics. Each element—whether it's an interactive quiz, emotionally driven story, eye-catching infographic, or engaging video—should complement the other aspects of your content strategy, creating a cohesive narrative that resonates with your audience on multiple levels. Through such thoughtful integration, you can craft a consistent brand message that not only attracts but retains audience interest and loyalty.

2.6 Final Thoughts

Creating engaging content that resonates with audiences is crucial for successful marketing strategies. This chapter explored various content types, including interactive posts, behind-the-scenes glimpses, and user-generated content, all designed to foster deeper audience connections and boost engagement. Through dynamic storytelling, brands can personalize experiences, build trust, and amplify credibility by sharing real-life testimonials and using relatable characters. The importance of video content was also highlighted as it offers opportunities for dynamic storytelling and better retention of information.

Incorporating these strategies requires a deep understanding of the target audience's preferences and behaviors. Entrepreneurs and small business owners should integrate these approaches into their content plans to build strong relationships and enhance brand loyalty. Meanwhile, marketing professionals and social media managers can refine digital strategies by leveraging these innovative tactics aligned with current trends. By effectively applying these methods, businesses can maximize their impact in the competitive landscape and ensure long-lasting relationships with their audiences.

Chapter 3: Building a Robust Brand Presence

E stablishing a robust brand presence is essential for success in today's competitive digital marketplace. With countless businesses vying for consumer attention, having a distinct and memorable brand identity can make all the difference. A strong brand presence involves more than just eye-catching logos or witty slogans; it requires an authentic and consistent approach that resonates with your audience on various platforms, especially social media. This chapter will delve into the strategies that can help you create and maintain such a presence, focusing on authenticity and consistency as key components in establishing your brand's unique voice. Understanding how to effectively communicate your brand's identity will not only attract customers but also foster long-term loyalty.

The chapter will explore several vital elements needed to build a solid online identity for your brand. It examines the importance of defining a consistent brand voice that aligns with your core values and mission, ensuring that every message you deliver is recognizable and trustworthy. Furthermore, you'll learn about creating cohesive messaging across different channels, which boosts brand recognition and enhances customer engagement. Additionally, regular audits and adjustments are discussed as necessary steps to ensure your brand remains aligned with its goals and resonates with its target audience. By adopting these approaches, entrepreneurs, marketing professionals, and social media managers will gain insights into crafting meaningful connections with their audience through effective social media marketing strategies.

3.1 Developing a Consistent Brand Voice

Building a robust brand presence in today's digital landscape requires a concerted effort to establish a consistent brand voice. This element is not merely a creative choice; it serves as a critical tool for fostering brand recognition and loyalty among audiences. Let's delve into why a consistent brand voice is important and how it can significantly enhance your brand's affinity with its audience.

Firstly, defining a distinct brand personality is fundamental to creating recognizable traits and tones that resonate across various channels. A brand personality encapsulates the unique attributes and ethos of a business, which should be consistently reflected in all forms of communication. For instance, a brand positioned as youthful and innovative will choose language and visuals that portray energy and modernity. This distinct personality helps audiences recognize and relate to the brand, as it projects consistency in character, much like meeting the same friend who always shows true colors in different settings.

Cohesive messaging across platforms is another pillar supporting brand trust and familiarity. In a world where consumers engage with brands through diverse media—social networks, emails, websites, and more—it's crucial to deliver a uniform message that aligns seamlessly across these touchpoints. Harmonizing the core message while adapting to each platform ensures that the audience receives a consistent brand experience, whether they are interacting with you on Instagram or reading an email newsletter. This strategy prevents confusion and builds confidence, as people lean towards brands that showcase reliability and straightforwardness in their communications.

Moreover, personality-driven communication has an emotional pull that resonates deeply with target audiences. When a brand stays true to its established personality, every interaction feels authentic and genuine. This authenticity strengthens the bond between the brand and its customers. For example, a brand known for its humor should maintain this tone even when addressing more serious matters, such as customer service inquiries or product announcements. By doing so, it not only entertains but also reassures the audience of its commitment to consistency, ultimately leading to greater engagement and loyalty.

Regular audits provide invaluable insights into maintaining alignment with the brand's voice and highlight areas for improvement. Tracking and analyzing content performance across channels can reveal inconsistencies or deviations from the established brand voice, offering opportunities for optimization. For instance, if certain social media posts receive less engagement, a review might indicate that the tone or messaging deviated from the expected brand personality. Conducting

these audits empowers brands to refine their communication strategies, ensuring every piece of content aligns closely with their brand identity and supports their goals.

An exemplary case study reinforcing the importance of brand voice consistency is during the 2008 recession when McDonald's maintained its advertising strategy steadfastly despite economic downturns. Unlike competitors who cut back, McDonald's sustained its messaging, projecting stability and reliability. This decision led to an increase in market share and underscored the power of consistency in branding. Customers gravitate toward brands that emit assurance and unwavering identity, even amidst uncertainty, reaffirming the connection trust has with a steady brand image.

Creating a consistent brand experience entails aligning every piece of communication with the overarching mission and values of the brand. This strategic alignment fortifies the brand's position and enhances its reputation. Every message disseminated must echo the brand's commitment to its core values, such as innovation or transparency. By embedding these principles into the brand voice, businesses ensure their content resonates authentically with the target audience, making each interaction meaningful and memorable.

3.2 Creating Brand Guidelines

Developing brand guidelines for language, tone, and style is essential to maintaining consistency across all forms of communication. These guidelines serve as a blueprint that helps align everyone involved in communicating on behalf of your brand. By establishing clear parameters, team members can be unified in their approach, ensuring that each interaction reflects the brand's core identity and values.

Consistency in brand communication is crucial for preventing customer confusion. When your audience receives mixed messages due to inconsistent communication styles, it may lead to misunderstandings about your brand's mission or offerings. A coherent brand message fosters familiarity, which in turn builds trust among customers. This makes them more likely to engage with your brand repeatedly. According to Liz Doig, a Brand Language Consultant at Wordtree, anchoring your brand's tone in its core values ensures that every piece of communication resonates with authenticity and sincerity.

One of the significant advantages of having well-defined guidelines is the simplification of the content creation process. With a clear framework in place, content creators can focus on generating ideas and crafting compelling narratives without spending excessive time deliberating over style or tone. This streamlines workflows and enhances productivity, enabling teams to produce consistent, high-quality content efficiently. Additionally, this clarity reduces revisions and inconsistencies, aligning the final output with the brand's objectives from the outset.

Maintaining these guidelines doesn't just stop at creation; regular training sessions are indispensable for equipping teams to represent the brand effectively. Training helps new members acclimate to the brand's tone and ensures that existing team members stay updated on any changes or evolutions in brand messaging. Such ongoing education empowers employees to embody the brand's voice confidently and consistently, no matter their role or the platform they are communicating through.

Creating comprehensive brand guidelines involves several key steps. Start by defining your core values, as these will inform the overall tone and style of your communications. Each piece of content should reflect these values, whether it's rigorous accuracy in reporting facts or a curious exploration of future trends. By rooting your communication style in your values, you create a unique and identifiable brand voice. This distinctiveness positions your brand to stand out in a crowded market, enhancing customer recall and engagement.

It's also important to assess your current brand and style guide regularly. This evaluation provides insights into how well your current communication practices align with desired outcomes. Reading sections of your website aloud, brainstorming adjectives to describe your tone, and collecting feedback from customers are all useful techniques for gauging your brand's current efficacy. Monitoring metrics like bounce rates and site engagement can also signal when adjustments are needed to better capture your audience's attention.

Once guidelines have been developed, ensure they are accessible and easy for all team members to understand. Complex jargon or convoluted instructions will only hinder implementation. Instead, use straightforward language and organize the document in a user-friendly manner. Highlight any key differences in tone that might apply to different channels or situations, such as social media versus formal business communications.

Another critical aspect is inclusivity. Your brand's tone should be welcoming to all audiences. Consulting inclusivity resources, like The Acrolinx Inclusive Language Guide, can help you craft a voice that is universally appealing while remaining true to your brand's identity. This consideration not only broadens your appeal but also underscores your commitment to diversity and representation, further strengthening your connection with your audience.

3.3 Cultivating an Authentic Online Persona

In the digital age, building an authentic online persona is crucial for businesses aiming to resonate with audiences and establish trust. This goes beyond mere marketing; it's about creating genuine connections that reflect the core values of your brand.

One effective method to achieve authenticity is by sharing real stories that enhance relatability and humanize the business. Consumers today crave authenticity and transparency. They want to know the people behind the brand, their journeys, struggles, and triumphs. By sharing these narratives, you not only provide a glimpse into the heart of your business but also create emotional touchpoints that can significantly impact audience engagement. Real-life stories make your brand relatable and accessible, bridging the gap between a faceless corporation and its customers.

Engagement is another pillar in developing an authentic on-line presence. Actively engaging with followers strengthens emotional bonds, transforming passive viewers into active participants in your brand's story. Responding to comments, participating in discussions, and acknowledging feedback are essential practices. Such interactions demonstrate that your brand values customer input, enhancing the relationship between you and your audience.

Highlighting team members is an excellent way to personalize and differentiate your brand. When you showcase your team, you're presenting the human side of your business. Intro-ducing the individuals who contribute to your brand adds layers of personality and differentiation. It also fosters a sense of community and inclusion, as audiences can relate to the diverse faces and stories within your team. This personal touch not only strengthens relationships with existing customers but also attracts potential clients looking for brands with authenticity and character.

Encouraging feedback and demonstrating responsiveness is vital in fostering loyalty. In today's fast-paced digital environ-ment, consumers expect quick and meaningful interactions. By actively seeking out customer opinions and promptly re-sponding to their concerns or compliments, you show that your brand values customer satisfaction. This openness to dialogue can lead to stronger loyalty, as customers appreciate brands that listen and adapt based on their input.

Moreover, consistent interaction builds long-term relation-ships as it creates a reliable channel of communication. It's about being present and available when your audience needs you most. This consistency establishes your brand as dependable, helping cement trust over time.

Through these practices, your online persona evolves from merely a voice on social media to a trusted partner in your customer's journey. It's essential to remember that authenticity isn't a trend—it's a commitment to honesty, transparency, and a genuine desire to connect with your audience.

3.4 Leveraging User-Generated Content

User-generated content (UGC) has become a cornerstone in building brand credibility and community in the digital landscape. By actively engaging customers in creating content, brands can establish a more authentic presence that resonates with audiences. UGC provides valuable social proof—a phenomenon where people rely on the opinions and actions of others to guide their behavior. When potential customers see real users sharing their experiences with a product or service, it builds trust and encourages engagement.

Brands that invite consumers to contribute content not only benefit from increased engagement but also bolster their reputation through authentic endorsements. As third-party content, UGC carries more weight with audiences because it's viewed as unbiased. Brands like Sugar Factory have successfully leveraged consumer-generated media, becoming widely recognized for their Instagrammable aesthetics that encourage patron participation without overt marketing pressure.

46

Once brands have prompted the creation of UGC, showcasing it across multiple platforms can further amplify customer voices. Social media platforms such as Instagram, Facebook, and Twitter serve as dynamic stages where businesses can display photos, reviews, and testimonials from satisfied customers. This approach not only expands reach but also deepens connections by highlighting authentic customer experiences, reinforcing trust and loyalty among the audience. By regularly updating these platforms with fresh UGC, businesses maintain relevance and offer engaging content that speaks directly to their target market.

Running UGC campaigns is another effective strategy to spark creativity and broaden brand exposure. These campaigns can take various forms—ranging from photo contests to hashtag challenges—encouraging customers to share their unique perspectives. Notably, user interaction in these campaigns often leads to viral moments, exponentially increasing a brand's visibility. For instance, a well-designed campaign that aligns with current trends can quickly capture public attention and expand reach beyond initial expectations.

To maximize the potential of UGC, creating a dedicated gallery for user contributions can help reinforce shared experiences and foster brand loyalty. Such galleries serve as a repository of positive interactions between the brand and its customers, creating a sense of community. They act as living testimonials, offering prospective customers a glimpse into what they might experience should they choose to engage with the brand. This visual representation of community involvement not only solidifies existing relationships but also attracts new followers who value transparency and genuine connections.

Regular audits of brand voice ensure the alignment and impact of UGC initiatives remain consistent with overall branding strategies. By periodically assessing the tone and representation conveyed through UGC, businesses can determine whether adjustments are necessary to maintain brand integrity and authenticity. This proactive approach enables companies to swiftly adapt to evolving consumer expectations while preserving the core elements of their brand identity, thereby cultivating a responsive and enduring brand presence.

3.5 Training Your Team

In today's competitive business landscape, equipping your team with the right training for effective brand representation is more essential than ever. Empowered teams not only enhance a company's brand image but also elevate customer interactions, driving engagement and loyalty.

Empowered teams are often at the forefront of creating positive brand perceptions. When employees are well-versed in the company's values, mission, and products, they project confidence and reliability to customers. This confidence translates into improved customer interactions as employees can effectively communicate and address queries, leading to increased satisfaction and trust in the brand. This process begins with comprehensive training programs that focus on instilling these core brand values across different roles within the organization.

Training plays a vital role in ensuring a unified approach both online and offline. For businesses operating in the digital age, consistency across all platforms—whether it be social media, email, or face-to-face interactions—is crucial. Training provides team members with a deep understanding of how to represent the brand cohesively, regardless of the medium. This consistency helps solidify the brand's identity, making it easily recognizable to consumers and fostering a sense of familiarity. A unified brand presence prevents mixed messages from confusing customers and ensures that everyone from sales personnel to customer service representatives can deliver the same message, reinforcing the brand's core values and promise.

In today's fast-paced environment, knowledgeable teams have an edge because they can adapt swiftly while maintaining the brand essence. Social media trends, consumer preferences, and market dynamics change rapidly, and only those teams equipped with adaptable skills and knowledge can keep up. Training that emphasizes critical thinking, problem-solving, and adaptability ensures that employees can respond to changes without losing sight of the brand's core identity. As a result, businesses can maintain relevance and competitiveness without sacrificing the principles that define their brand.

Feedback mechanisms are another integral aspect of building an empowered team. Businesses that incorporate regular feedback sessions as part of their training protocols not only optimize internal understanding but also improve execution. Feedback provides employees with insights into their performance and highlights areas for improvement, fostering personal and professional growth. Moreover, open feedback channels encourage idea-sharing and innovation, empowering employees to contribute actively to the brand's evolution. These mechanisms create a culture of continuous improvement, where employees feel valued for their contributions and motivated to maintain high standards.

Implementing systematic feedback processes enables companies to identify potential gaps in their training programs and address them proactively. By listening to employee experiences and challenges, organizations can refine their training approaches to align better with real-world scenarios, thus enhancing the overall effectiveness of training initiatives.

For instance, role-playing exercises that simulate real-life customer interactions can be incorporated into training sessions. These exercises help employees practice and refine their communication and problem-solving skills, preparing them to handle diverse situations with ease and confidence. Such practical application of learned skills reinforces theoretical knowledge and ensures that employees are ready to represent the brand authentically and consistently.

Moreover, creating avenues for employees to share success stories and best practices can significantly enhance team motivation and performance. Celebrating achievements and acknowledging the efforts of individuals who embody the brand's essence not only boosts morale but also inspires others to strive for excellence.

The strategic implementation of training programs is a fundamental component of building a strong, cohesive team capable of driving a brand's success. It involves understanding the unique needs of each team member and tailoring training sessions to address these needs effectively. Businesses should consider using diverse training methodologies, such as e-learning modules, interactive workshops, and mentorship programs, to cater to varying learning preferences and ensure maximum engagement.

Furthermore, ongoing training is essential to keeping employees updated with the latest industry trends and practices. Regularly scheduled training sessions focusing on emerging technologies, new marketing strategies, and changing consumer behaviors help bridge the gap between current capabilities and future requirements. Continuous education ensures that team members remain competent and motivated, ready to tackle any challenges that come their way.

To measure the impact of training initiatives, companies must establish clear metrics and benchmarks. Tracking employee performance before and after training sessions helps quantify the effectiveness of these programs. Additionally, using tools such as surveys and feedback forms allows organizations to gather valuable insights into employee satisfaction and the perceived value of the training received.

By investing in comprehensive training programs, businesses empower their teams to become strong advocates for their brand. Trained employees understand the importance of aligning their actions with the company's goals and values, resulting in a consistent and authentic brand representation across all touchpoints. This alignment not only enhances the brand's reputation but also contributes to long-term customer loyalty and business growth.

Masterly Consulting Group exemplifies this approach, offering specialized social media training designed to empower employees while adhering to the company's social media policy. Moreover, as endorsed by the Association for Talent Development, such training focuses on building skill sets that enable employees to represent the brand effectively, whether through virtual or direct interactions.

3.6 Final Thoughts

In this chapter, we've explored how establishing and maintaining a consistent brand voice is crucial for building a strong online presence. By defining and adhering to a distinct brand personality, businesses can create a recognizable identity that resonates with their audience across various digital platforms. The importance of unifying messages throughout social media, emails, and other touchpoints helps in preventing confusion while fostering trust and familiarity among consumers. We've seen how an authentic approach, even when addressing serious matters, strengthens connections with customers, resulting in increased engagement and loyalty.

Furthermore, developing comprehensive brand guidelines ensures that all stakeholders involved in communication uphold the brand's core values like innovation or transparency. Regular audits and training sessions keep the team aligned with these principles, allowing them to adapt swiftly to changing trends without losing sight of the brand essence. By leveraging user-generated content, brands can enhance credibility and community, showcasing genuine customer interactions that resonate with potential clients. Through consistency in tone and strategic interaction, your brand can transform from being just another name to a reliable partner in your customer's journey.

Chapter 4: Driving Engagement Through Interaction

Driving engagement through interaction on social media is a strategic endeavor that requires thoughtful planning and execution. By leveraging interactive strategies, brands can enhance user participation and build stronger connections with their audiences. In an era where digital presence directly influences business success, understanding how to engage users effectively on social media platforms can elevate one's brand visibility and customer loyalty. The dynamics of social media are ever-changing, presenting both challenges and opportunities for businesses to connect with their audience in meaningful ways. Interaction is more than just a buzzword; it is the key to converting casual followers into devoted advocates who help spread brand messaging organically.

This chapter delves into various methods and techniques for increasing user engagement through interaction. Readers will explore the importance of crafting effective calls-to-action (CTAs) that inspire users to take specific actions like sharing content or making a purchase. The chapter also covers the significance of engaging with comments and messages to build community relationships and establish a loyal customer base. Additionally, hosting live events and Q&A sessions are discussed as innovative ways to enhance real-time interaction and keep audiences actively involved. Finally, the chapter emphasizes the role of feedback in creating compelling content that resonates well with followers and encourages consistent participation. By understanding these components, entrepreneurs, marketing professionals, and social media managers can implement practical strategies to drive engagement and foster vibrant online communities, ultimately supporting their growth objectives.

4.1 Implementing Effective Call-to-Actions (CTAs)

In the digital age, Call to Actions (CTAs) have become essential tools for maximizing user engagement on social media platforms. Strategically crafted CTAs can transform passive viewers into active participants, helping businesses and marketers alike foster a more dynamic interaction with their audience. The role of CTAs in enhancing user interaction cannot be overstated, as they leverage urgency and psychological triggers that prompt immediate action from users.

One of the most effective ways CTAs boost interaction is by harnessing the power of urgency and psychological cues. Urgency acts as a powerful motivator because people generally don't want to miss out on limited-time offers. A CTA such as "Get 20% Off Today Only!" creates an immediate need to act, compelling users to take advantage of what seems like a fleeting opportunity. Similarly, incorporating social proof within a CTA – like "Join 10,000 Satisfied Customers" – can build trust and encourage potential customers to follow suit by capitalizing on the herd mentality that drives many purchasing decisions.

To further enhance user engagement, CTAs must be clear, concise, and personalized. Clarity ensures that users precisely understand the action required, while conciseness keeps the message from becoming overwhelming or diluted. Personalized CTAs, tailored to specific user behaviors or preferences, can significantly increase the likelihood of engagement. Imagine seeing a CTA that reads, "Hi [Your Name], unlock exclusive content just for you!" This not only addresses the user directly but also implies a unique opportunity tailored to them, which can dramatically improve response rates.

One practical guideline for creating effective CTAs involves ensuring they align closely with audience interests and needs. By using language and offers that resonate with the target demographic, CTAs can effectively guide users toward desired actions. For example, a fitness brand might craft a CTA like "Start your fitness journey today with a free trial!" This aligns with the prospective customer's desire to improve health and fitness, encouraging them to engage immediately.

The effectiveness of CTAs can also be amplified by tailoring them to fit the dynamics of different social media platforms. Each platform has its own features and user behaviors, necessitating a customized approach. On Facebook, for instance, the use of carousel ads allows multiple CTAs, engaging users with a variety of products. A fashion brand might use distinct CTAs like "Shop Now" on each item in a carousel ad, directing users to product-specific pages. This strategy maximizes the reach and appeal of the brand's offerings by catering to varied user interests all at once.

On LinkedIn, a professional-oriented platform, CTAs should focus on career advancement or industry insights. For example, the CTA "Download the Report" in sponsored content can entice professionals seeking to gain valuable knowledge, thereby boosting lead generation. This aligns smoothly with LinkedIn's user intent, making it highly effective for B2B marketing efforts.

Analyzing successful CTA examples can provide invaluable insights into strategic wording and design. For instance, Twitter's fast-paced environment favors brief and direct CTAs, such as "Retweet to Enter" during contests. This type of CTA capitalizes on Twitter's social sharing nature, exponentially increasing the visibility and engagement of the post with each retweet. Additionally, using Twitter Polls with the CTA "Vote Now" invites immediate interaction, feeding users' curiosity and providing brands with instant feedback.

Delving into these examples highlights key elements such as proper placement, color contrast, and verb choice – all crucial components in designing effective CTAs. When a CTA button stands out visually yet complements the overall branding, it naturally draws the user's eye, leading to higher conversion rates. Colors evoke emotions and actions, so selecting appropriate palettes is essential; for example, red can induce feelings of urgency, promoting quicker decision-making.

Moreover, A/B testing different versions of CTAs is vital in determining the most effective combination of elements for a particular audience. Testing variations in color schemes, placement, sizes, and wording helps identify what resonates best, optimizing CTA performance across different campaigns and platforms.

Ultimately, the art of crafting compelling CTAs lies in balancing creativity with a deep understanding of audience psychology and behavior. Every detail, from the wording to the visual presentation, plays a significant role in guiding users through the conversion funnel. For small business owners, entrepreneurs, and marketing professionals, refining CTA strategies can translate into enhanced brand presence, increased engagement, and, consequently, more conversions.

4.2 Engaging with Comments and Messages

Active engagement on social media is a cornerstone for building meaningful relationships and fostering community loyalty. In an increasingly digital world, genuine interactions can set businesses apart by creating a lasting impression on their audience. Timely responses to comments and messages are integral to this process, as they show the audience that their input is valued and respected. Responding quickly not only satisfies users but can also enhance a brand's image, making followers feel appreciated and heard.

For many businesses, the difference between retaining a loyal customer base and losing potential clients lies in how swiftly and sincerely they address their followers' concerns and inquiries. Studies have shown that a significant percentage of social media users expect brands to reply within a short time frame. Meeting these expectations demonstrates a commitment to customer satisfaction and prioritizes the audience's needs over internal processes. According to Eckstein, actively responding to customer service requests on social media significantly boosts brand favorability. This highlights the importance of being present and ready to engage at all times.

Personalizing interactions is another vital aspect of fostering active engagement. This goes beyond generic replies and involves using names or crafting responses that cater to individual experiences and contexts. Such personalization transforms engagements into authentic exchanges, making followers feel special and acknowledged. A simple gesture like addressing someone by their first name or recalling a previous interaction can leave a lasting positive impact, embedding an emotional connection between the brand and its audience. Brands that successfully implement personalized communication often enjoy higher levels of consumer trust and loyalty, which translates into long-term business success.

Furthermore, utilizing feedback from comments is a valuable tool for shaping future content. Feedback provides insights into what the audience enjoys or dislikes, allowing businesses to adjust their strategies accordingly. By acknowledging and implementing user feedback, companies demonstrate their willingness to adapt and evolve in alignment with their audience's interests. This ongoing dialogue creates a more engaging atmosphere where the audience feels invested in the brand's narrative. Based on Barnhart, promptly addressing customer feedback improves satisfaction and fosters brand loyalty, underscoring the importance of this dynamic approach.

Building a community through active interaction also requires highlighting user contributions and hosting discussions. Recognizing audience efforts by sharing their content or achievements encourages more participation and promotes a sense of belonging within the community. Social media platforms are ideal venues for such activities, as they allow for diverse expressions and facilitate constructive dialogues. Inviting followers to participate in discussions about shared interests strengthens community bonds and nurtures a collaborative environment where everyone's voice matters. These interactions form the foundation of a thriving online community, one characterized by mutual respect and shared enthusiasm.

Hosting regular discussions or forums where followers can express opinions and share experiences further enhances community engagement. By creating spaces for open dialogue, businesses not only gain deeper insights into their audience's preferences but also establish themselves as approachable entities willing to listen and learn. This approach reinforces the idea of community ownership, encouraging members to take an active role in the development and growth of the collective space. It transforms passive observers into active contributors, thereby fostering a culture of inclusivity and shared responsibility.

4.3 Hosting Live Events and Q&A Sessions

Real-time events, particularly live streaming and interactive sessions, have emerged as powerful tools for driving audience engagement on social media platforms. By creating an opportunity for immediate interaction, these events not only attract large viewership but also deepen the connection between brands and their audience. Here's how facilitating meaningful engagement through real-time events can transform your social media strategy.

Promoting live events effectively is crucial to ensuring that your audience shows up prepared and engaged. Clear communication about what viewers can expect, how they can participate, and why it matters to them sets a positive tone before the event begins. Leveraging various channels like emails, social media posts, and even personal invitations can help maximize turnout. Setting expectations regarding content, duration, and interaction opportunities ensures that viewers come with a mindset ready for engagement. Establishing clear objectives and sharing them with potential attendees can align interests and heighten anticipation, as seen in many successful campaigns.

During the event, fostering an interactive atmosphere through questions or polls is key to keeping audiences actively involved. This strategy taps into the human desire for participation and belonging, transforming a passive viewing experience into a dynamic conversation. Live polls, especially, offer a simple yet effective way to capture instant reactions and keep the energy high. Statistics show that incorporating live polling can significantly increase participant involvement and satisfaction. Beyond engagement, these interactions yield valuable insights into audience preferences, which can be pivotal in tailoring future events and marketing strategies. Audience questions during the events not only personalize the experience but also create a sense of co-creation as viewers contribute to the dialogue.

The momentum should not end when the event does. Post-event follow-ups are crucial in maintaining engagement and extending the conversation's life span. Sharing highlights, key takeaways, and recorded sessions keeps the audience connected and provides value long after the event concludes. This approach also allows those who couldn't attend live to engage at their convenience, further broadening your reach. Reflecting on feedback gathered during the event and communicating any changes or future plans based on this input demonstrates a commitment to active community involvement and can enhance brand loyalty.

To maximize the impact of real-time events, broadcasting across multiple platforms is an essential strategy. Different platforms cater to diverse user demographics and preferences, so adopting a multi-platform approach ensures broader reach and accessibility. For example, Instagram might appeal more to a younger demographic, while LinkedIn could engage professionals looking for industry-specific insights. Each platform offers unique tools and features that can enhance the event experience, from Instagram's Stories for quick updates to YouTube's capabilities for longer broadcasts. Utilizing these varied channels optimizes exposure and interaction opportunities, allowing for a customized and inclusive audience experience. This strategy aligns with the need to cater to an increasingly mobile and global audience, breaking down geographical and technological barriers.

4.4 Using Feedback for Content Creation

Audience feedback is a vital component for enhancing content strategy on social media platforms. By effectively leveraging this feedback, businesses can tap into new ideas, improve their interactions, and ultimately meet their audience's needs more effectively.

Engaging with audience comments not only helps in building a connection but also provides fresh perspectives that can inspire future posts. Comments from the audience often reflect diverse opinions, experiences, and expectations, acting as an informal but rich source of market research. For instance, a travel blog may receive comments about destinations visitors are eager to explore or challenges they face while traveling. Such insights could lead to creating content like detailed guides on lesser-known destinations or tips on solo travel, directly addressing the audience's interests and concerns. This process of mining comments for content inspiration ensures that your posts remain relevant and resonate well with your followers.

Furthermore, responsive interaction with negative feedback plays a crucial role in identifying areas of improvement. Negative feedback should not be viewed merely as criticism but as constructive input from which lessons can be learned. Engaging thoughtfully with such feedback demonstrates a company's commitment to quality and customer satisfaction. For example, if customers express dissatisfaction with the complexity of an online tutorial, acknowledging their concerns and simplifying future instructions conveys a willingness to adapt. This approach not only rectifies the specific issue at hand but also builds trust as it showcases the brand's dedication to delivering valuable content.

Collecting suggestions and opinions systematically provides guidance for content direction and aids in refining strategies. Implementing structured feedback collection methods, such as surveys or polls, allows brands to gather focused data on what the audience specifically wants to see. Questions targeting preferences, like "What topics would you like us to cover next?" or "Which format do you prefer: video or articles?" can yield actionable insights. These user-driven initiatives enable brands to align content creation with audience demands, ensuring that the material remains engaging and effective.

Integrating audience feedback into content showcases a willingness to adapt and meet audience expectations, solidifying the relationship between the brand and its followers. This practice involves openly sharing how feedback has influenced changes or innovations within the content strategy. For instance, a tech company might announce updates to its online resources based on customer suggestions, detailing enhancements like quicker loading times or more intuitive navigation. Such transparency not only validates the audience's input but also fosters a sense of co-creation, where followers feel valued and part of the brand's evolution. This engagement model enhances loyalty and encourages ongoing participation, essential for sustainable content success.

To establish a proactive communication style that builds trust, consider deploying a systematic approach to feedback management. Creating a dedicated feedback loop allows consistent evaluation and utilization of audience insights, ensuring that their voices are heard and acted upon. Additionally, actively engaging audiences directly through interactive elements— such as Q&A sessions, webinars, or live chats—can prompt further involvement and foster a collaborative community atmosphere. Direct engagement encourages more participation as audiences see their contributions being acknowledged and appreciated.

Incorporating audience feedback should not be seen as a one-off task but as an integral aspect of content strategy. Continuously reviewing and adapting based on feedback ensures relevance and effectiveness in reaching target goals. As social media landscapes evolve, staying attuned to audience needs through regular feedback collection and implementation strengthens content strategies, ensuring they remain dynamic and aligned with the evolving desires of the audience.

4.5 Building Community through Interaction

In today's digital landscape, the value of a thriving online community cannot be overstated. For businesses and marketers striving to make impactful connections on social media, fostering a sense of belonging is essential. This sense of belonging encourages increased engagement and contributes to the overall success of the brand's presence online.

One effective way to foster community is by regularly high-lighting user comments and contributions. When people see their input acknowledged, they feel valued and become more inclined to interact. It creates a ripple effect; recognition not only boosts the morale of one individual but also encourages others to engage. Acknowledging contributions publicly can take various forms, such as featuring user-generated content, sharing testimonials, or even spotlighting insightful comments. This practice fosters a culture of appreciation and emphasizes that every voice matters in the community.

Equally important is hosting discussions around shared interests. These dialogues serve as a meeting point for like-minded individuals, enhancing the bond within the community. Discussing common topics allows followers to connect over mutual passions, whether it's debating industry trends or sharing personal experiences related to a niche interest. Platforms such as Facebook groups or Reddit threads can serve as ideal venues for these discussions, providing spaces where users can dive deep into subjects without the pressure of traditional social media dynamics. Such interactions turn passive followers into active participants, strengthening the ties within the community and building a solid foundation of trust and camaraderie.

Recognizing and rewarding active community members can further cement this sense of belonging. Incentives play a crucial role in encouraging ongoing participation. Rewards could range from small gestures, such as thank-you notes or social media shoutouts, to more substantial offerings like exclusive content access or special discounts. By implementing a structured recognition program, businesses signal their appreciation, motivating members to remain involved and contribute consistently. Recognition doesn't only benefit the awarded individuals but acts as an encouragement for others to increase their involvement, knowing their efforts might also be appreciated.

Creating a welcoming communication environment is another cornerstone for cultivating a loyal audience community. Inclusivity should be at the heart of all interactions, ensuring that every member feels seen and heard. This requires creating clear guidelines that promote respectful dialogue and discourage any form of harassment or exclusion. Establishing norms for interaction can set the tone and maintain a positive atmosphere, encouraging ongoing engagement. Community managers play a vital role here by modeling inclusive behaviors and stepping in when necessary to mediate conflicts or clarify misunderstandings.

An inviting communication climate helps establish a safe space where all opinions are valued, and members are encouraged to share openly without fear of judgment. Using friendly language, being approachable, and showing genuine interest in the community's needs are simple yet effective strategies to foster such an environment. Additionally, utilizing feedback loops where community suggestions are actively sought and implemented also demonstrates commitment to collective growth, reinforcing the community's loyalty.

Furthermore, interactive activities such as polls, Q&A sessions, and collaborative projects can significantly enhance community engagement. They provide opportunities for real-time interaction and involve members in decision-making processes, further embedding them in the community fabric. For example, a brand might use Instagram's polling feature to decide on future products or initiatives, allowing followers to have a say in the company's direction. This participatory approach empowers members, making them feel integral to the brand's journey.

Particularly for entrepreneurs and marketing professionals, understanding these dynamics opens pathways to build authentic relationships with their audience, ultimately translating into business advantages. The emotional connection formed through these community-building efforts often results in higher customer retention, increased word-of-mouth referrals, and a more robust brand reputation. Businesses that position themselves as more than just service providers, but as community leaders and connectors, enjoy a strategic advantage in today's competitive market.

4.6 Final Thoughts

In this chapter, we've explored how interactive strategies, specifically through the implementation of effective call-to-actions (CTAs), can significantly enhance user engagement on social media platforms. By understanding and applying principles like urgency, psychological triggers, and personalization, businesses can transform passive viewers into engaged participants. These tactics are essential for small business owners and marketing professionals who aim to create a dynamic interaction with their audience. The examples provided underscore the importance of aligning CTAs with platform dynamics and audience preferences, ensuring that each call to action resonates with its intended target.

Moreover, this chapter has highlighted the power of engaging directly with comments and messages to build community loyalty and foster genuine relationships. Timely and personalized interactions, as well as the strategic use of feedback, contribute to stronger brand presence and customer satisfaction. Entrepreneurs, marketers, and social media managers can leverage these insights to not only enhance user engagement but also cultivate a thriving online community. The methods discussed serve as a guide to creating meaningful connections, helping brands to establish trust and encourage ongoing participation from their audience.

Chapter 5: Converting Followers into Customers

Transforming followers into customers is a key focus in today's digital marketing landscape. With social media playing an increasingly central role in business strategies, understanding how to navigate this transition is essential for success. As brands continue to build their presence online, engaging with followers isn't enough; the goal is to establish a deeper relationship that translates into tangible business results. This chapter offers insights into strategic approaches necessary for this conversion process. It guides readers through the foundational aspects of gaining trust and cultivating interest among followers, setting the groundwork for turning casual engagement into committed customer relationships.

The chapter delves into a variety of tactics centered around social media and digital marketing, designed to convert social media followers into loyal customers. Readers will explore the art of crafting compelling lead magnets, which are instrumental in capturing the attention and contact information of potential customers. Effective use of these tools can help build a significant database of leads eager to learn more about your offerings. Additionally, the chapter discusses ways to create persuasive offers that entice followers to take the next step in the purchasing journey. It emphasizes designing targeted ad campaigns tailored to resonate with specific audience segments, thus enhancing the relevance and impact of your messages. Retargeting strategies are also examined, showing how they can be used to re-engage users who have shown initial interest but haven't yet converted. Finally, the importance of ongoing monitoring and performance improvement of marketing efforts is highlighted, providing actionable steps to optimize your strategies continually. Through these insightful sections, the chapter equips marketers, entrepreneurs, and social media managers with effective strategies and skills necessary to boost customer acquisition from existing followers.

5.1 Creating Compelling Lead Magnets

In the realm of digital marketing, lead magnets play a pivotal role in converting social media followers into loyal customers. They work as enticing offers that exchange valuable content or services for contact information, making them indispensable tools for building a robust customer database. For entrepreneurs, marketers, and social media managers aiming to grow their brand presence, understanding and leveraging lead magnets effectively is crucial.

Lead magnets act as the bridge between attracting an audience and converting them into paying customers. By offering something of perceived value in exchange for contact details, businesses can create a database of potential leads to nurture and convert over time. This process not only expands your reach but also targets individuals who have already shown interest in what your brand has to offer. The data collected helps tailor future communications to these prospects, aligning your offerings with their specific needs and preferences. As a result, this enhances the likelihood of conversion from mere interest to completed purchase.

One of the most impactful ways to generate interest through lead magnets is by addressing specific pain points of your target audience. By understanding the challenges and desires your prospects face, you can craft lead magnets that resonate deeply with them. This alignment builds trust and positions your brand as a source of valuable solutions, laying the groundwork for a strong initial relationship. An effective lead magnet should offer clear, actionable insights or solutions to pressing problems, demonstrating your commitment to helping your audience succeed. For instance, a consulting company might provide a free guide on overcoming common industry challenges, showcasing both expertise and empathy towards its audience's struggles.

Diverse types of lead magnets can be employed to capture different segments of your audience. E-books, white papers, and guides are excellent choices for showcasing expertise and establishing authority in your field. These thorough resources demonstrate a deep understanding of complex topics, inviting users to delve deeper into your specialized knowledge. On the other hand, simpler formats like checklists, templates, or cheat sheets can offer quick wins for those looking for immediate results. These provide practical value without requiring significant time investment from your prospects, catering to audiences looking for speedy solutions.

Free trials and demos are another powerful form of lead magnet, particularly for service-based businesses and software companies. Offering prospects a firsthand experience of your product allows them to test its features and benefits before committing financially. This hands-on approach not only builds confidence in your product's capabilities but also provides concrete reasons for potential customers to move forward with a purchase decision. For example, a SaaS company could offer a two-week trial period for its software, allowing users to explore its functionalities and witness its impact on their daily operations.

The effectiveness of a lead magnet is significantly influenced by how well it aligns with the unique selling proposition (USP) of your brand. A compelling USP captures attention and highlights what makes your offering stand out from competitors. Including elements of your USP within your lead magnet ensures that prospects immediately recognize the distinctive benefits of engaging with your brand. This approach not only attracts more qualified leads but also fosters stronger brand recall and loyalty. For instance, if your business prides itself on eco-friendly practices, creating a lead magnet that focuses on sustainable solutions would resonate well with environmentally conscious prospects.

Crafting a compelling lead magnet requires careful consideration of its content and presentation. It should offer substantial value, whether through educational insights, practical advice, or exclusive access to premium resources. The presentation should be professional and engaging, employing visuals and design elements that enhance readability and appeal. Additionally, the call-to-action associated with your lead magnet must be clear and persuasive, encouraging prospects to take the desired step of sharing their contact information. An optimized call-to-action not only improves conversion rates but also ensures that prospects understand the immediate benefits they'll receive by opting in.

Promoting your lead magnet effectively is key to maximizing its reach and impact. Utilize multiple channels such as social media, email marketing, and website pop-ups to draw attention to your offer. Social media, in particular, provides an excellent platform for reaching a broad audience while enabling targeted promotions based on user interests and behaviors. By segmenting your audience and tailoring your messaging accordingly, you can ensure that your lead magnet resonates with the right individuals at the right time. Additionally, consider incorporating testimonials or case studies within your promotional materials to build credibility and trust among prospective leads.

5.2 Crafting Compelling Offers

Creating an enticing lead magnet is crucial for converting followers into customers. It serves as a gateway, drawing potential clients in with the promise of value while subtly encouraging them to engage further with your brand. Let's explore how you can craft attractive and persuasive lead magnet offers that resonate with your audience.

A strong headline is the first impression your audience will have. Its importance cannot be overstated, as it significantly impacts engagement decisions. A well-crafted headline clearly communicates what the reader can expect from the lead magnet and why it's beneficial to them. Incorporating power words like "Ultimate," "Proven," or "Guaranteed" can create a sense of urgency and anticipation. Using numbers adds clarity and sets expectations, keeping the promise precise and compelling. For instance, "5 Steps to Transform Your Social Media Strategy" provides both intrigue and a clear benefit.

Design plays a pivotal role in how your lead magnet is perceived. An eye-catching, professional design enhances the perceived value, making your offer more appealing. The cover should reflect high-quality graphics and align with your brand's visual identity. Tools like Canva or Visme can help create stunning visuals. Alternatively, hiring a graphic designer ensures a polished look that stands out in any setting. Imagine your lead magnet displayed at a trade show; a well-designed cover is likely to attract attendees, capturing their interest amid numerous options.

Highlighting benefits and potential results within your lead magnet can create a sense of urgency and drive conversion rates higher. It's essential to articulate what advantages users gain from engaging with your content. Phrases such as "Discover strategies that increased leads by 20% in one month" pique curiosity and set clear expectations. This approach clarifies why sharing contact details is valuable, transforming curiosity into actionable interest. Including testimonials or case studies can further enhance perceived value. Real-world examples where your lead magnet has made a difference solidify its authenticity and relevance, encouraging new users to follow suit.

To maximize engagement, ensure your lead magnet is easily digestible. Busy entrepreneurs and professionals appreciate straightforward, concise information that respects their time. Utilize bullet points, short paragraphs, and visual elements to break down complex ideas, making them accessible and engaging. A "Key Points" summary at the end of each section not only reinforces the main takeaways but also serves as a quick reference guide for future interactions, enhancing the overall user experience.

Incorporating a powerful call-to-action (CTA) at the end of your lead magnet is vital. This is your chance to turn interest into tangible action. Whether it's subscribing to a newsletter or booking a demo, the CTA should be clear, compelling, and direct. Words that inspire immediate action are most effective here, urging readers to move forward with confidence. Testing various formats, like checklists or video tutorials, can help identify what resonates best with your audience, allowing you to adapt your strategy accordingly.

Furthermore, offering your lead magnet in multiple formats caters to different learning preferences. Some might prefer a detailed guide, while others are drawn to succinct checklists. Providing options increases the likelihood of engagement, as users will gravitate towards the format that suits their style. This flexibility implies a deeper understanding of your audience's needs, positioning your brand as adaptable and considerate.

Tackle specific issues your audience faces to ensure your lead magnet resonates deeply. In a saturated content environment, generic offerings often go unnoticed. Rather than broad topics, focus on niche areas that directly address your audience's concerns. For example, instead of a general "Social Media Strategies" guide, opt for something targeted like "5 Proven Techniques for Boosting Engagement on Instagram." Such precision in addressing problems demonstrates deep insight into your audience's challenges and portrays your brand as knowledgeable and attentive.

Delivering high-quality content is non-negotiable. The caliber of your lead magnet reflects your brand's expertise and reliability. Ensure the content goes beyond superficial insights, providing meaningful, actionable value. Instead of mere overviews, delve into specifics backed by industry research or case studies, demonstrating a comprehensive understanding of the topic. This approach not only builds trust but positions your brand as an authoritative voice in your field.

Finally, consider embedding social proof elements within your lead magnet. Testimonials from satisfied users, detailed case studies, endorsements from industry experts, or impressive user statistics can make your offering more credible. Such proof reassures potential clients about the effectiveness and popularity of your lead magnet, reducing hesitation and building confidence in your brand's capabilities.

5.3 Designing Targeted Ad Campaigns

Creating ads that effectively capture attention and drive conversions is essential for businesses aiming to transform followers into loyal customers. One of the most effective strategies to enhance ad performance involves audience segmentation, which is crucial in increasing ad relevance and minimizing wasteful spending.

Audience segmentation involves dividing your broader audience into smaller, more targeted groups based on specific criteria such as demographics, interests, or purchasing behavior. By doing this, businesses can tailor their adverts to meet the unique needs and preferences of each segment. For instance, a company selling eco-friendly products might create distinct ads for environmentally-conscious millennials and another set for parents concerned about sustainability. This approach ensures that the message resonates with each group's values and lifestyle, leading to higher engagement and conversion rates. It also minimizes waste by ensuring that ads are only shown to those most likely to be interested in them, thus optimizing marketing budgets.

Next, focusing the ad copy on benefits rather than features is another powerful strategy. While it's common to highlight what a product does, emphasizing the benefits it offers the consumer creates a stronger emotional connection and urges action. For example, instead of saying "Our software has advanced analytics," you might highlight how using this software will simplify data management and boost sales through real-time insights. This benefit-oriented approach speaks directly to the consumer's needs, addressing pain points and offering solutions, thus making the ad more compelling and actionable.

This leads us to the significance of high-quality visuals in advertising. Visuals are processed by the brain much faster than text and have the power to evoke emotions instantly, making them a critical component in capturing attention. Using vibrant colors that align with your brand's identity can evoke desired emotions, while high-resolution images or professional graphics enhance the perceived quality of your ad. For instance, a clothing brand showcasing its new collection will benefit from crisp, well-lit photos that display the fabric's texture and color vibrancy. These visual elements play a crucial role in making the ad attractive enough to interrupt scrolling and prompt consumers to learn more.

Branding consistency across all ads reinforces trust and recognition among your audience. Maintaining a consistent visual style, including logos, color schemes, and fonts, helps build a cohesive brand image that audiences can easily identify. For example, Apple's minimalistic yet sophisticated visual style is recognizable across its various platforms and campaigns. This consistency not only strengthens brand recall but also reinforces the brand's promises and values, fostering trust among potential customers.

Implementing these strategies requires a balance between creativity and strategic planning. Businesses should not shy away from experimenting with different formats and ideas to find what resonates best with their target audience. It's vital to stay updated with the latest trends and consumer behaviors, which can provide fresh insights into crafting engaging content. Combining data-driven decisions with creative storytelling ensures ads remain relevant and impactful.

Furthermore, businesses should leverage advanced targeting options offered by advertising platforms to reach the most receptive audience segments. Features like lookalike audiences and demographic targeting can help ensure that ads are shown to individuals with similar behaviors or characteristics as your existing customer base. Retargeting past visitors who didn't convert initially can also be highly effective in maintaining brand visibility and nudging them closer to a purchase decision.

Integrating gamified experiences or interactive elements within ads can significantly enhance user engagement. Incorporating challenges, rewards, or virtual try-ons can make ads more dynamic and enjoyable, thus encouraging interaction. For example, a fitness app could include an interactive challenge in its ad to motivate users to engage with the content and explore the app further. Similarly, augmented reality (AR) features allow users to visualize products in real-world settings, aiding decision-making and providing a unique experience.

Lastly, monitoring ad performance through robust analytics is crucial for ongoing improvement. By tracking key metrics and conducting A/B testing, businesses can gain insights into what content and formats resonate most with their audience. Adjustments based on these insights lead to higher returns on investment and reduced cost per click, ultimately making ad campaigns more efficient and successful.

5.4 Utilizing Retargeting Strategies

Retargeting is a powerful digital marketing strategy designed to re-engage users who have previously interacted with your brand but stopped short of completing a desired action, such as making a purchase. This approach is key to maintaining brand visibility and converting interested prospects into loyal customers by reinforcing your brand presence in the minds of potential buyers.

One of the main advantages of retargeting is its ability to keep your brand at the forefront of potential customers' minds. When users visit a website and browse through products without making a purchase, they may later encounter ads for those same products while visiting other websites or using social media platforms. This consistent exposure ensures that your brand remains relevant and top-of-mind, increasing the likelihood of conversions when these users are ready to make a decision. By continuously reminding users of the products they have shown interest in, businesses can significantly increase their chances of turning these past interactors into paying customers.

Dynamic ads play a crucial role in enhancing conversion chances. These ads are personalized and show users the specific products they viewed previously on your site. For example, if someone explored various models of smartphones but didn't complete a purchase, a dynamic ad might remind them of the exact model that caught their eye. This tailored approach taps into the user's existing interest, encouraging them to return to your site and complete the purchase. The use of dynamic retargeting ensures that ads are directly relevant to each user's prior behavior, effectively nudging them down the conversion path. As these ads focus on items already familiar to users, they inherently possess a higher chance of capturing attention and prompting action than generic advertisements.

Moreover, personalizing ads based on user behavior not only increases engagement but also helps reduce hesitation towards purchasing. Personalized ads create a sense of relevance and connection with the prospective customer, addressing their unique preferences and behaviors. For instance, if a user has previously shown interest in eco-friendly products, serving them an ad highlighting the green credentials of a product can resonate deeply, aligning the brand's offerings with the user's values. Such personalization fosters a stronger emotional connection with potential customers, which is essential for building trust and alleviating any concerns they might have about proceeding with a purchase. Additionally, by showcasing features, discounts, or benefits tailored to the individual's browsing habits, brands can effectively diminish barriers to conversion and encourage decisive steps towards buying.

The strategic implementation of retargeting involves several steps to ensure maximum efficiency and effectiveness. Firstly, understanding your audience is paramount. Segmenting users based on their interactions with your website allows you to tailor your advertising efforts more precisely. Whether it's identifying visitors who left products in their shopping carts or those who viewed a particular category multiple times, segmentation enables businesses to craft more relevant ad experiences. This segmentation helps distinguish between

82

different levels of buyer intent and craft messages that speak directly to each segment's experiences and reasons for leaving the site without purchasing initially.

Another critical component of successful retargeting lies in continuously testing and refining your campaigns. Utilizing A/B testing methods on ad creatives, messaging, and timing can provide insights into what resonates most with your audience. It allows marketers to optimize their strategies continuously, ensuring that they deliver the most impactful ads. Monitoring key performance indicators such as click-through rates, conversions, and return on ad spend is vital in this process. By evaluating these metrics, businesses can identify successful tactics and areas needing improvement, ensuring optimal resource allocation and increased return on investment.

In addition to leveraging digital tools like tracking pixels, which help monitor user behavior across the web, integrating AI and machine learning technologies can further enhance retargeting efforts. These technologies can predict consumer behavior based on historical data, allowing marketers to anticipate and respond to user needs proactively. By employing predictive analytics, companies can streamline the retargeting process, delivering highly customized content that aligns with the user's journey in real-time.

5.5 Monitoring and Improving Campaign Performance

In the realm of social media marketing, converting followers into loyal customers requires strategic planning and execution. A critical aspect of this process involves measuring and optimizing campaign effectiveness. By focusing on these elements, entrepreneurs, marketing professionals, and social media managers can significantly enhance their strategies and yield better returns on investment.

To start, tracking metrics is essential for optimizing campaigns and gauging how audiences interact with content. Metrics provide valuable insights that guide decision-making processes, helping marketers understand which aspects of their campaigns resonate most with their audience. For example, evaluating clicks, impressions, and engagement rates enables marketers to identify successful tactics and areas needing improvement. These metrics are vital indicators that reveal the efficacy of an advertisement in terms of reach, interest generation, and overall engagement levels. They offer a clear view of whether the current strategy is effective or requires adjustments.

Once metrics are identified and tracked, A/B testing becomes an invaluable tool for refining content and formats that appeal to the target audience. This controlled experimentation allows marketers to test different variations of ads or posts to see which version yields better results. A/B testing informs decisions by showing what messages, images, or calls-to-action engage or convert followers more effectively. By comparing outcomes from these tests, marketers gain a deeper under-standing of what drives consumer behavior, enabling them to tailor content more precisely to meet audience preferences.

After identifying what works best through continuous test-ing and analysis, the next step involves adjusting campaign elements based on newfound insights. These tweaks ensure that marketing investments yield higher returns by enhancing performance metrics like ROI and reducing costs per click (CPC). Optimizing creative elements, such as headlines or visuals, and strategic components like ad placement or timing can make a significant difference. For instance, if a particular format outperforms others in engagement but costs are high, adjust-ments might include tweaking visual quality or distribution strategies to balance reward and expenditure.

Moreover, it is important to emphasize that real-time mea-surement and adjustment are crucial for maintaining the com-petitiveness of a campaign. The dynamic nature of social media landscapes demands that marketers remain agile, continuously analyzing data and reacting to shifts in audience behavior and market conditions. This proactive approach not only helps maintain the relevance of marketing campaigns but also enhances their effectiveness over time. By leveraging real-time data, marketers can fine-tune their strategies promptly, ensuring that campaigns remain aligned with business goals and audience expectations.

In addition to these strategies, utilizing advanced tools and technologies can further enhance campaign effectiveness. For example, employing analytical tools that provide comprehensive reports on key performance indicators (Kpis) allows marketers to dive deeper into campaign data. These reports help dissect various metrics like conversion rates, customer lifetime value, and cost-per-acquisition, offering detailed insights that drive smarter decision-making. Additionally, automation tools can streamline the process of tracking and analyzing metrics, freeing up time for marketers to focus on creative aspects and strategic planning.

Ultimately, the goal of measuring and optimizing campaign effectiveness is to foster deeper connections with audiences while achieving business objectives efficiently. By systematically tracking metrics, conducting A/B tests, and adjusting elements based on insights, businesses can create more impactful social media strategies. These practices enable marketers to allocate resources more effectively, achieve higher engagement rates, and convert followers into loyal customers successfully.

5.6 Final Thoughts

In this chapter, we explored a variety of strategies to effectively transform social media followers into loyal customers. By focusing on creating compelling lead magnets, we've seen how these tools can bridge the gap between mere interest and customer conversion. This approach emphasizes addressing specific pain points of target audiences, underlining the importance of aligning offerings with their needs and preferences.

Additionally, we discussed the use of different types of lead magnets – from e-books and white papers to free trials and demos – to cater to diverse audience segments. The significance of a well-defined unique selling proposition (USP) in making lead magnets more compelling was also highlighted, showcasing how tailored content that resonates with users' values can enhance engagement and brand loyalty.

Crafting enticing offers through strong headlines, appealing design, and clear calls-to-action was another key focus. We've learned how promoting these lead magnets across various channels, like social media and email, can maximize reach and effectiveness. Furthermore, understanding what elements appeal to your audience by testing different formats and including testimonials or case studies can further bolster trust and interest. Through consistent efforts in refining these tactics, entrepreneurs, marketers, and social media managers can build stronger connections with their audiences, resulting in increased brand presence and customer conversion.

Chapter 6: Leveraging Influencer Partnerships

L everaging influencer partnerships offers a strategic avenue for brands to extend their reach and boost customer engagement on social media. In today's digitized landscape, influencers serve as powerful conduits between brands and target audiences. They possess the unique ability to not only amplify brand messages but also lend authenticity that resonates in ways traditional marketing approaches often cannot achieve. Collaborating with well-aligned influencers allows brands to tap into established trust and credibility, fostering deeper connections with potential customers who are increasingly turning to social media for product recommendations and insights. Successful influencer partnerships can transform brand perception, making them an invaluable component of effective social media strategies.

As you delve into this chapter, you'll discover practical guid-ance on selecting influencers who align with your brand values and mission. The discussions will illuminate the process of identifying niche influencers whose specialized knowledge and audience rapport make them particularly valuable. You'll learn about evaluating engagement metrics to distinguish between influencers based not just on follower count but on genuine interactions with their audience. This chapter will walk you through the nuances of authenticity in content alignment, ensuring that partnerships feel natural and credible to both the influencer's followers and your intended market. Additionally, the text explores the role of digital tools and platforms in streamlining influencer discovery and collaboration, emphasizing efficiency in aligning influencer characteristics with your campaign objectives. Ultimately, this chapter equips you with the essential skills needed to execute meaningful partnerships that drive tangible business results.

6.1 Identifying the Right Influencers for Your Brand

In the rapidly evolving world of social media marketing, selecting influencers who resonate with your brand values and target audience is a crucial strategy for fostering genuine connections and driving successful campaigns. A well-chosen influencer acts as a bridge between your brand and potential customers, providing authenticity and credibility that traditional advertisements often lack.

Understanding Niche Influencers

To select influencers aligned with your brand, begin by identifying those within niches related to your brand's mission and values. Niche influencers have honed their expertise and following in specific areas, making them more relatable and trusted by their audiences. For instance, if your brand promotes sustainable living, connecting with eco-conscious influencers who advocate for environmental causes can enhance your outreach. This synergy ensures that both the influencer's audience and your brand's message are harmoniously intertwined, leading to higher engagement levels. Understanding and leveraging these niche influencers can be instrumental in achieving conversion rates that surpass efforts aimed at broader audiences.

Evaluating Engagement Over Follower Count

While an influencer's follower count may initially seem like a measure of potential reach, it's essential to delve deeper into engagement metrics. High follower counts do not always equate to active participation. Analyze metrics such as likes, comments, and shares to gauge true engagement. An influencer with a smaller, engaged community is often more valuable than one with millions of passive followers. Such influencers can foster meaningful discussions and interactions around your brand, spurring genuine interest and customer loyalty. According to recent findings, influencers who maintain consistent rapport with their audience can significantly impact brand perception and drive more effective campaign results.

Authenticity and Content Alignment

The authenticity of an influencer's content is vital when determining their suitability for your brand. In today's digital landscape, consumers are adept at recognizing insincere endorsements. Partnering with influencers who seamlessly incorporate your brand into their authentic storytelling enhances credibility and trust. Examine past collaborations and current content to ensure a natural fit with your brand ethos.

Influencers who genuinely appreciate your product or service will convey this enthusiasm to their followers, leading to more impactful and resonant partnerships.

For example, beauty brands benefit immensely from collaborations with influencers who possess a genuine passion for makeup. The authenticity of their recommendations translates to higher conversion rates and a stronger brand presence. By aligning with influencers whose values and interests mirror your own, your brand's message becomes an integral part of an engaging narrative rather than a commercial interruption.

Streamlining Discovery with Influencer Platforms

Navigating the vast expanse of social media influencers requires efficient tools and strategies. Utilizing influencer discovery platforms like Upfluence or Influencity can simplify the process, offering access to databases categorized by interests, engagement rates, and content style. These platforms enable marketers to filter candidates based on specific criteria, ensuring alignment with brand values and objectives. Additionally, employing social listening tools helps track relevant keywords and hashtags, allowing brands to identify influencers actively discussing topics pertinent to their industry.

These digital solutions facilitate meticulous research, eliminating guesswork while saving time and resources. By prioritizing value alignment and audience resonance over sheer numbers, businesses can forge partnerships with influencers whose audiences are most likely to engage with and become advocates for their brand.

Guideline: Researching Previous Collaborations

It's beneficial to research an influencer's previous collaborations as part of the selection process. Analyzing how they have partnered with other brands can provide insight into their working style, professionalism, and audience response. This background check is pivotal for ensuring that their values remain consistent and that their audience aligns with your target demographics.

By focusing on influencers whose past engagements reflect positively on your brand, you mitigate risks associated with potential reputation damage and maximize the likelihood of a successful partnership. An influencer's history of consistent, credible collaborations often indicates their ability to foster lasting impacts on consumer perception and brand trust.

6.2 Negotiating Influencer Agreements

Forging win-win agreements with influencers is crucial for businesses seeking sustained relationships and successful campaigns. Collaborations with influencers can propel a brand's reach, but to achieve mutual success, it's essential to lay a solid foundation through well-defined agreements. A clear agreement not only minimizes misunderstandings but also builds trust that fosters long-term partnerships.

First and foremost, defining deliverables with specificity is pivotal. In influencer marketing, ambiguity often leads to missed expectations. Clearly outlining what is expected from the influencer ensures both parties are on the same page.

This includes detailed descriptions of content types, frequency of posts, platforms to be used, and any branding guidelines that need to be adhered to. By agreeing upon these elements at the outset, all stakeholders can work towards common goals without confusion or conflict. Furthermore, establishing performance metrics and success indicators in advance helps in assessing campaign effectiveness, setting realistic targets, and providing feedback for continuous improvement.

Compensation structures form another critical aspect of influencer partnerships. Monetary payments are straightforward, but exploring other forms of compensation such as performance incentives can be beneficial. For instance, bonuses tied to engagement rates or conversions can motivate influencers to invest more effort in promoting your brand. Such incentives ensure that influencers remain committed to delivering high-quality content that resonates with their audience, aligning their success with yours. Performance-based compensation encourages innovation and creativity, fostering a partnership where both parties reap rewards proportional to their contributions. It's vital to negotiate compensation plans thoughtfully, taking into account the influencer's reach, engagement, and the potential return on investment for your brand.

Understanding legal considerations is equally important in crafting robust influencer agreements. Adhering to Federal Trade Commission (FTC) guidelines ensures transparency and compliance, protecting both the brand and the influencer from legal repercussions. Clear disclosure of sponsored content maintains authenticity and trust with the audience. Additionally, discussing content ownership rights upfront prevents disputes over intellectual property. The contract should specify whether the brand or the influencer retains ownership of the created content, and under what circumstances it can be reused or repurposed. These legal frameworks safeguard against potential misuses and reinforce the professional nature of the partnership.

Building long-term relationships is at the heart of sustainable influencer collaborations. Loyalty programs can be an effective tool in achieving this, rewarding influencers for their continued association with your brand. Such programs might offer benefits like early access to new products, exclusive events, or higher commission rates over time. By showing appreciation for their ongoing support, brands can strengthen loyalty and encourage influencers to become genuine advocates. Open communication is another cornerstone of lasting partnerships. Regular updates, feedback sessions, and collaborative brainstorming build rapport and foster an environment where both parties feel valued and heard. It's crucial to maintain transparency regarding campaign performance, sharing insights and data that can help influencers optimize their approach and align better with brand objectives.

Incorporating a structured approach to engagement assessment is also beneficial. Tools that analyze metrics like likes, comments, shares, and overall engagement rate provide insights into the influencer's performance and audience interaction. These tools can help you select influencers whose audiences are actively engaged, ensuring your message reaches those most likely to convert into customers. Monitoring these metrics consistently enables brands to make informed decisions about continuing or revising collaboration terms based on influencer performance, ensuring that partnerships remain productive and aligned with strategic goals.

Likewise, forging connections with influencers who authentically resonate with your brand amplifies campaign impact. Influencers who genuinely align with your brand values communicate more authentically, leading to increased audience trust and engagement. Long-term partnerships with such influencers can cultivate loyal communities around your brand, driving sustained interest and conversion over time. Commitment to nurturing these relationships through personalized interactions and shared values fosters a sense of belonging, encouraging influencers to invest in your brand's success.

6.3 Measuring the Impact of Influencer Marketing

To assess the effectiveness of influencer partnerships in expanding your brand's reach and boosting engagement, adopting a data-driven marketing approach is essential. This strategy enables businesses to make informed decisions grounded in real-time data insights and analytics, helping optimize marketing efforts and maximize return on investment.

One foundational step towards achieving this is establishing key performance indicators (KPIs) that align with your campaign goals. Identifying these KPIs allows marketers to measure progress and make necessary adjustments to strategies almost instantaneously. For example, if the objective is to increase brand awareness, metrics like social media impressions and follower growth rates become crucial. Meanwhile, for campaigns focused on increasing sales, conversion rates and customer acquisition costs may be more relevant. By setting clear, actionable KPIs, businesses can ensure that their influencer collaborations are effectively contributing to broader marketing objectives.

In addition to KPI establishment, tracking engagement and reach through comparative analysis plays a pivotal role in refining influencer selection. This involves assessing how different influencers perform in terms of audience interaction and content dissemination. Tools like Google Analytics or social media insights provide valuable data on aspects such as click-through rates, shares, and comments. Comparing these metrics across different influencers offers a clearer picture of who truly engages their audience and amplifies your message. It's crucial to view an influencer's success beyond surface-level metrics like follower count, as genuine engagement often leads to stronger brand impact.

To complement quantitative measurements, gathering qualitative feedback can deepen understanding and guide messaging adjustments. Feedback collected from both influencers and the target audience can reveal nuanced insights into audience sentiment and responsiveness to campaigns. Conducting surveys or encouraging direct conversations with followers can provide richer context to the numbers, helping identify what resonates or falls flat. Qualitative insights are invaluable in shaping the tone and content of future campaigns, ensuring they connect authentically with intended audiences.

Monitoring conversion rates through unique tracking methods provides tangible evidence of an influencer partnership's business impact. Setting up customized links, promo codes, or dedicated landing pages can help trace back conversions directly to specific influencer campaigns. This detailed tracking method assesses the direct effect of the influencer's content on consumer behavior, showcasing the tangible outcomes of these partnerships. A high conversion rate indicates successful alignment between influencer messaging and audience needs, while low rates may suggest misalignment or areas needing improvement.

Furthermore, integrating sophisticated tools like predictive analytics and artificial intelligence can enhance decision-making processes. These technologies utilize historical data to forecast future outcomes, empowering marketers to anticipate trends and adjust strategies proactively. Predictive models help refine influencer selection by identifying those likely to drive desired consumer behaviors based on past performance patterns. When applied correctly, these insights lead to more effective, targeted campaigns that reach the right audience at the right time.

It's also worth noting that overcoming challenges in maintaining data quality and ensuring team literacy in data tools is essential for successful data-driven marketing. Without accurate data, decisions become misguided, potentially risking campaign outcomes. Training marketing teams in data comprehension and tool usage ensures everyone involved can accurately interpret insights and utilize them effectively.

6.4 Understanding Niche Influence

When it comes to enhancing brand outreach, leveraging the dedicated followings of niche influencers can be a game-changer. Engaging with these influencers allows brands to connect with audiences who trust their recommendations and are more likely to engage actively. The key lies in identifying those niche influencers whose followers see them as credible sources, thereby increasing the potential for heightened engagement.

The first step is selecting the right niche influencers. These are individuals who have carved out a space within specific markets and developed a loyal follower base that values their opinions and insights. This dedication translates into a higher level of trust when the influencer recommends products or services, which naturally leads to increased engagement. According to Dan, collaborating with influencers boasting engaged audiences generates better interaction rates, typically ranging from 3% to 5%. By recognizing influencers whose followers value their authenticity, brands can align themselves with trusted voices that elevate their message.

Collaboration with such influencers isn't just about engagement; it's also about conversion rates. Brands should focus on those who effectively target appeals to their audience, thus driving tangible results. As Brandbassador suggests, targeted content sparks conversation and excitement, leading to enhanced conversion opportunities. Micro-influencers within niche markets often generate significantly higher conversion rates compared to broader campaigns because their promotions resonate more personally with their audience. They understand what makes their followers tick and use this knowledge to craft messages that appeal directly to those needs and interests.

However, it's vital to take a close look at the influencer's history of collaborations. Reviewing past partnerships can provide valuable insights into how they align their values with the brands they endorse. Ensuring alignment between the influencer's ethos and your brand's values is crucial for maintaining authenticity and credibility. When both parties share aligned missions and principles, it creates a seamless partnership that resonates well with the audience. This synergy not only strengthens the campaign's impact but also fosters long-term relationships built on mutual respect and understanding.

This leads us to the importance of engaging with niche-specific content. Influencers who regularly create content within their specific niches are not only seen as experts by their audience but also contribute to fostering authentic connections. By crafting messages that speak directly to the unique interests and concerns of their followers, these influencers build stronger bonds with their audience, creating a sense of community and shared passion. For brands, partnering with such influencers implies gaining access to an audience that values sincerity and honesty over superficial metrics.

Utilizing influencer platforms can further enhance the efficacy of these partnerships. Platforms designed specifically for influencer marketing streamline processes and provide analytics to assess influencers' past performance, helping to make informed decisions about potential collaborations. Understanding the features of these platforms enables brands to efficiently discover influencers who not only fit their niche but also complement their values and branding objectives.

Ultimately, leveraging the power of niche influencers means tapping into a network of dedicated followers who trust and rely on their recommendations. It's about moving beyond numbers and focusing on meaningful interactions that drive real business outcomes. By carefully selecting the right influencers, reviewing their previous collaborations, and embracing niche-specific content, brands can form authentic connections that resonate deeply with audiences, resulting in increased engagement and conversions.

6.5 Engagement Beyond Numbers

In influencer marketing, the value of genuine audience interaction takes precedence over superficial metric counts. While many brands are entranced by influencers with massive followings, a more strategic approach lies in valuing small influencers who boast high engagement rates. These influencers, often referred to as micro-influencers, tend to have a more profound connection with their audience. This connection translates into higher levels of trust and authenticity—a crucial component for effective marketing.

Micro-influencers engage their audience in meaningful ways, fostering loyalty and driving conversations that matter. Their followers are more likely to be genuinely interested in their content and, consequently, the products they promote. Therefore, brands can vastly benefit from partnering with these smaller yet highly engaged influencers as opposed to those with larger followings but low interaction levels. This strategy not only enhances brand credibility but also optimizes marketing budgets by focusing on quality rather than quantity.

Moreover, tools and technologies play a pivotal role in analyzing active audience responsiveness. Mere presence is insufficient when real engagement is what truly matters. Advanced analytic tools enable marketers to delve deeper into metrics like likes, comments, and shares, offering valuable insights into whether an influencer's audience is actively engaging with their content or merely observing passively. By utilizing these tools, brands can differentiate between real and effective audiences, thereby making informed decisions when selecting influencers for collaborations.

The alignment of audience demographics with target market objectives is another critical facet. A successful influencer partnership hinges on ensuring that the influencer's audience matches the brand's ideal customer profile. For instance, if a brand aims to appeal to young, tech-savvy individuals, teaming up with an influencer known for creating content around technology and gadgets would be advantageous. This alignment ensures coherence in campaign efforts and maximizes the potential for reaching the right people who are more likely to convert into loyal customers.

To obtain this alignment, brands should thoroughly research potential influencers' audience demographics using available data. Understanding aspects such as age, location, interests, and purchasing behavior helps tailor campaigns that resonate with the intended audience. When the audience feels personally connected to the content, engagement naturally increases, paving the way for enhanced brand recognition and potential sales growth.

Furthermore, prioritizing influencers who maintain consistent interaction with their followers is a wise course of action. Influencers who routinely engage with their audience through comments, replies, and direct messages build a strong rapport and foster a sense of community. This ongoing interaction not only boosts trust but also ensures that the influencer remains relevant in a rapidly evolving digital landscape.

Consistency in engagement reflects an influencer's dedication to nurturing relationships with their followers, which is a quality that brands should seek when forming partnerships. By collaborating with such influencers, brands can tap into loyal fan bases that are more inclined to respond positively to endorsements and recommendations. This consistent interaction often leads to heightened brand awareness and increased conversion rates, ultimately providing a substantial return on investment for the brand.

To solidify these strategies, it's essential for brands to establish clear guidelines and expectations with their chosen influencers. Defining deliverables with specificity minimizes misunderstandings and sets the stage for transparent and effective collaborations. By outlining campaign goals, content requirements, and engagement expectations upfront, both parties can work towards achieving mutually beneficial outcomes.

6.6 Final Thoughts

In this chapter, we delved into the strategic importance of collaborating with social media influencers to enhance brand reach and boost engagement. We discussed how choosing the right influencers—those who align with your brand's values and target audience—can make a significant difference in campaign success. By focusing on niche influencers who resonate with specific market segments, businesses can form genuine connections that lead to higher engagement and conversion rates. We also emphasized the value of evaluating engagement over follower counts, as true interaction is more indicative of an influencer's impact. Authenticity in content and alignment with brand ethos are key factors for establishing trust and credibility with audiences.

Furthermore, we explored practical tools and strategies to streamline influencer discovery and selection, ensuring partnerships that echo brand objectives and appeal to desired demographics. By leveraging these insights, entrepreneurs, marketing professionals, and social media managers can make informed decisions that effectively amplify their brands' messages. The chapter highlighted the role of clear agreements in forging sustainable relationships with influencers, underscoring the mutual benefits of well-structured collaborations. With this knowledge, readers are better equipped to navigate the complex landscape of influencer marketing, driving successful outcomes and fostering lasting.

Chapter 7: Harnessing Analytics for Success

H arnessing analytics is a vital aspect of modern social media marketing success. It involves understanding and utilizing data to make informed decisions that enhance both engagement and sales. In an era where digital footprints are as revealing as they are plentiful, leveraging analytics tools can set the trajectory for a brand's growth and outreach. These tools act as navigational beacons, guiding entrepreneurs, marketing professionals, and social media managers through the vast ocean of data towards achieving their strategic objectives. Data-driven insights help in crafting content that resonates with the audience, ensuring every post not only reaches but interacts meaningfully with potential customers. Understanding the nuances of social media dynamics helps in maintaining a competitive edge and fostering sustainable relationships with audiences.

In this chapter, readers will explore how specific analytics tools can be effectively utilized to measure and optimize social media efforts. The discussion will cover key performance indicators (KPIs) like engagement rate, conversion rate, reach, impressions, and follower growth rate. Each metric provides unique insights that contribute to comprehensive evaluations of marketing performance. Additionally, the chapter delves into methods of interpreting social media metrics and adjusting strategies based on data insights, emphasizing the importance of aligning analytics with broader marketing goals. By focusing on these areas, readers will gain valuable knowledge on implementing analytics tools to maximize engagement and drive sales, ultimately crafting data-driven strategies that foster brand growth and customer loyalty. With practical insights and actionable advice, the chapter aims to equip entrepreneurs, marketers, and managers with the skills needed to navigate the ever-evolving social media landscape confidently.

7.1 Key Performance Indicators (KPIs) in Social Media

In today's digital landscape, understanding key performance indicators (KPIs) is crucial for crafting effective social media strategies that drive engagement and sales. Tracking these metrics not only allows businesses to measure their current performance but also provides insights into necessary adjustments for achieving marketing goals. Among the essential KPIs are Engagement Rate, Conversion Rate, Reach and Impressions, and Follower Growth Rate, each offering unique insights into different aspects of social media performance.

Engagement Rate is a vital metric that reflects how well content resonates with an audience. It is calculated by assessing the number of likes, shares, and comments relative to the total number of followers or viewers. High engagement rates signify that the content successfully captures the audience's attention and encourages interaction. For example, a small business posting engaging content about its products may notice in-creased comments and shares, indicating strong interest and advocacy from its community. This engagement can further amplify reach when algorithms on platforms like Facebook or Instagram recognize active interactions, subsequently pro-moting the content to more users. High engagement not only enhances visibility but also sends positive signals to social media algorithms, thus expanding a brand's potential audience.

Conversion Rate is another critical KPI that measures the effectiveness of converting social media engagements into desired actions, such as sales or sign-ups. By calculating the percentage of interactions that result in a conversion—whether it be making a purchase or subscribing to a newsletter—businesses can gauge the success of their lead nurturing efforts. Tracking this metric allows businesses to assess the return on investment (ROI) of their social media campaigns, highlighting the importance of aligning content with broader marketing objectives. Analyzing data over time can reveal patterns, such as which types of posts or promotions yield the highest conversion rates, allowing marketers to refine their strategies accordingly.

Reach and Impressions provide insight into the number of users exposed to content, which is particularly valuable for evaluating resource allocation and optimizing strategies. Reach refers to the total number of unique users who view content, while impressions account for the total number of times content is displayed, regardless of clicks. These metrics are important for understanding the potential impact of a post and whether it's effectively reaching the target audience. For instance, a campaign with high impressions but low engagement might indicate that while many users see the content, it's not compelling enough to encourage interaction. Such insights can prompt businesses to experiment with different content types or messaging to better capture audience interest.

Follower Growth Rate is a key indicator of brand interest and influence. Monitoring the pace at which a brand gains new followers provides insights into audience expansion and can help assess the effectiveness of broader brand awareness efforts. A steady increase in followers often signals growing brand appeal and relevance. However, if follower growth stalls, it may signal the need for strategic adjustments to boost engagement and attract new audiences. Businesses can use this metric to identify periods of rapid growth or decline and correlate these trends with specific campaigns or content initiatives. Understanding these patterns helps inform future strategies and ensures continuous improvement in audience outreach.

For entrepreneurs and small business owners looking to expand their social media presence, maintaining a focus on these KPIs is integral to tracking progress and adapting strategies. Each metric offers unique insights, facilitating comprehensive evaluations of marketing performance. By understanding and leveraging these indicators, businesses can create data-driven approaches that resonate with their target audience, ultimately enhancing engagement and driving sales.

Marketing professionals seeking to enhance their skills can benefit from a keen awareness of how these KPIs interconnect. Crafting strategies that prioritize high engagement and conversion rates while maximizing reach and impressions leads to sustainable brand growth. Understanding the nuances of these metrics enables marketers to tailor content that not only attracts but also converts and retains customers.

Social media managers aiming to refine their tactics can leverage these insights to stay competitive in the ever-evolving digital landscape. Employing a strategic approach to monitoring KPIs ensures that content continues to meet audience expectations, fostering lasting relationships and brand loyalty. Through ongoing analysis and refinement, social media managers can capitalize on emerging trends and maintain a dynamic online presence that aligns with industry best practices.

7.2 Interpreting Social Media Metrics

Decoding social media analytics is crucial for any business aiming to enhance its marketing strategies. To transform raw data into actionable insights, one must first understand the context in which this data exists. Social media metrics do not exist in a vacuum; they must be closely aligned with broader marketing goals. For example, if increasing brand awareness is a primary objective, then tracking follower growth and reach becomes essential. These metrics can help businesses assess whether their efforts are resulting in greater visibility.

Understanding Data Context involves more than just recognizing what numbers indicate; it's about correlating these metrics with specific objectives. If the intent is to drive website traffic, for instance, analyzing referral traffic from social media channels will reveal how successful campaigns are in directing potential customers to your site. This correlation helps in making sense of the data, ensuring that it is used effectively to make informed decisions and optimize marketing strategies.

Benchmarking is another valuable approach. It allows businesses to measure their performance against industry standards or past achievements. By setting realistic goals based on these benchmarks, businesses can identify areas of underperformance early. Suppose a competitor's engagement rate is notably higher; this discrepancy could signal the need to revamp content strategies or explore new posting times. Benchmarking serves as a reality check, providing clarity on where improvements are necessary.

In addition to understanding context and benchmarking, Visualizing Data through graphs and charts significantly aids comprehension. Visualization makes it easier to spot patterns and trends within the data. For instance, a line graph displaying engagement rates over time can quickly show whether recent changes in strategy resulted in increased interaction. Not only does visualization simplify complex data, but it also enhances communication among team members, facilitating collaborative strategy adjustments.

Utilizing tools like Sprout Social, which offers advanced analytics, can further enhance data visualization capabilities. The ability to create customizable reports allows marketers to tailor their analysis, focusing on particular metrics that matter most to their business objectives. Visual tools serve as a bridge between raw data and strategic decision-making, allowing teams to act swiftly on insights gained.

Another critical component of decoding analytics is Identifying Trends. Social media is dynamic, with user preferences and engagement methods constantly evolving. Recognizing emerging trends enables businesses to adjust their strategies proactively. Trendspotting, such as identifying which types of content resonate most with audiences or which platforms are gaining popularity, ensures that marketing efforts remain relevant and effective.

Furthermore, social media analytics helps discover rising influencers or popular topics within an industry, which could be pivotal for forming collaborations or creating targeted content. By spotting these trends early, businesses position themselves as leaders rather than followers in their market. An example could be noticing a shift towards video content over static images, prompting a timely transition to more video-centric marketing approaches.

Incorporating trend analysis into regular strategy evaluations supports ongoing improvement and adaptation. Keeping an eye on both platform-specific developments and broader social media trends is vital for maintaining competitive advantage. Utilizing third-party tools like Hootsuite Analytics for comprehensive monitoring across multiple platforms can provide deeper insights into these trends.

Overall, decoding social media analytics requires a multi-faceted approach where understanding data context, benchmarking against industry standards, visualizing data, and identifying trends come together. Through these processes, businesses can turn superficial numbers into profound insights, crafting data-driven strategies that promote engagement and drive sales.

7.3 Adjusting Strategy Based on Data Insights

Incorporating data insights effectively into social media strategies is essential for businesses aiming to optimize their marketing efforts and drive better outcomes. A crucial aspect of this is embracing data-driven decision making, which involves continuously assessing and adapting strategies based on the information gathered from analytics. This allows businesses to remain agile and responsive in a fast-evolving digital landscape. To incorporate this approach, companies should first encourage a culture of learning and experimentation. By doing so, they can harness the full potential of their data resources, ensuring that decisions are not based solely on intuition or past experiences but are informed by actual performance metrics and results.

A key component of data-driven decision making is A/B testing, a method used to evaluate the effectiveness of different content variations. Through this process, marketers can determine which versions of their posts generate more engagement or conversions. For example, by testing two different headlines on a Facebook advertisement, businesses can identify which headline performs better in terms of click-through rates. The version that yields higher engagement can then be implemented more broadly. This iterative method of testing and optimizing content ensures that marketing strategies are continually refined and improved based on hard evidence rather than guesses. It is critical that businesses document the results of these tests to inform future campaigns and investments, maximizing their return on investment over time.

Feedback loops play an indispensable role in embedding continuous improvement into social media strategies. These involve reviewing the outcomes of marketing campaigns systematically to facilitate iterative enhancements. Implementing effective feedback loops requires overcoming challenges like data silos, where important datasets are restricted within separate organizational units. To address this, businesses must strive for seamless data flow across departments—integrating marketing, development, and operations teams—and ensure high data quality to avoid misleading conclusions. Additionally, balancing speed with insight is vital; while rapid iterations are advantageous, they must not compromise thoughtful analysis of user experiences and business results.

Moreover, the development of iterative strategies is necessary for remaining competitive. This approach embraces evolving methods driven by engagement patterns and insights gleaned from analytics. In practice, this means regularly updating and refining strategies to align with emerging trends and consumer behaviors. Consider a social media manager who notices a surge in video content consumption over static images in recent analytics reports. By adjusting the content strategy to focus more on video production, the manager can capitalize on this trend, thus optimizing engagement levels and driving desired actions. This cycle of constant adaptation not only keeps brands relevant but also ensures that marketing objectives are consistently met.

For instance, evaluating performance metrics such as user interactions, shares, and comments helps identify what resonates most with audiences. This data informs the creation of more engaging content, tailored specifically to audience preferences. Similarly, understanding the nuances of customer segments through psychographic analysis—such as identifying health-conscious individuals or outdoor enthusiasts—enables businesses to craft messages that speak directly to these groups' interests and values. This level of personalization enhances the likelihood of interaction and conversion, ultimately improving the efficacy of social media campaigns.

To implement these practices effectively, businesses need to foster a collaborative culture that values data literacy and transparency. Training employees on how to interpret analytics and apply insights to strategic decisions will empower teams to make informed choices that align with overarching business goals. It is also imperative to invest in robust analytics tools that can handle large volumes of data, offering actionable insights in real-time. Encouraging cross-functional teamwork and communication ensures that marketing strategies reflect diverse perspectives, ultimately leading to more holistic and effective approaches.

Finally, it is important for businesses to establish clear guidelines for conducting A/B tests and managing feedback loops.

For A/B testing, setting clear parameters, such as the variables to test and the duration of each test, will ensure reliable results. Organizations should maintain detailed documentation of previous tests to build on past learnings and avoid duplicating efforts. When creating feedback loops, integrating automated data validation and cleaning processes will improve data accuracy and reliability. Establishing regular review sessions post-campaigns to analyze data, discuss findings, and strategize improvements will foster a culture of continual growth and innovation.

7.4 Implementing Analytics Tools

Harnessing the power of analytics tools in social media marketing is essential for entrepreneurs, small business owners, marketing professionals, and social media managers aiming to enhance their strategies. As digital landscapes evolve, selecting appropriate analytics tools becomes crucial for making informed, data-driven marketing decisions that can boost engagement and drive sales.

The first step in leveraging analytics tools is choosing ones aligned with your business's specific needs and objectives. There are myriad options available, each serving different purposes. For instance, SEO tools like Ahrefs, SEMRush, and Moz are invaluable for improving website rankings on search engines. On the other hand, marketing attribution tools such as Amplitude and Twilio Segment organize audience interaction data, revealing the effectiveness of marketing efforts. The key to selecting the right tool lies in understanding what you aim to achieve—whether it's enhancing your search engine visibility or evaluating your marketing campaign's reach.

Once you've selected suitable tools, the next focus should be integrating them seamlessly with your existing marketing systems. This integration is vital for streamlining data collection and analysis, allowing for a consolidated view of your marketing performance. By connecting these tools with platforms managing customer interactions and content distribution, businesses can ensure real-time data flow, which aids in timely decision-making. For example, linking your analytics tools with CRM systems can provide comprehensive insights into customer behavior, helping tailor marketing strategies to meet evolving consumer demands.

Leveraging advanced features offered by analytics tools can also provide deeper insights into customer behavior. Modern analytics platforms come equipped with capabilities that go beyond basic data collection. They enable businesses to delve into predictive and prescriptive analytics, thus providing foresight into future trends and customer preferences. By utilizing these advanced features, marketers can better understand their audience's journey, segment customers more effectively, and develop personalized marketing campaigns that resonate with individual preferences, thereby enhancing engagement rates and conversion metrics.

However, it's not sufficient to integrate and use analytics tools without continuous evaluation. The landscape of marketing technology is ever-evolving, with new features and updates regularly emerging. To stay competitive, businesses must periodically assess the effectiveness of their analytics tools, ensuring they remain up-to-date with technological advancements. Adopting a proactive approach towards tool evaluation involves examining whether current tools meet your objectives or if there are updated alternatives that offer improved functionalities. Ongoing assessment helps in identifying gaps and enables swift adaptation to the latest market trends, thereby maintaining a strategic edge.

Moreover, ongoing evaluation should also consider the scalability and usability of the tools. As companies grow, their data needs expand. Therefore, selecting tools that can scale alongside business growth ensures that extensive data volumes can be managed without compromising on speed or accuracy. Tools should be user-friendly to allow easy navigation for team members with varying levels of technical expertise. This promotes efficient use and empowers teams to leverage analytics independently, fostering a data-driven culture within the organization.

While the process of selecting tools, integrating them with marketing systems, utilizing advanced features, and conducting ongoing evaluations might seem exhaustive, the benefits far outweigh the efforts. An optimized analytics strategy not only improves campaign targeting and effectiveness but also increases return on investment by allowing for more efficient resource allocation. Gaining this competitive advantage provides valuable insights into market trends and competitor strategies, positioning businesses well ahead in the race to captivate their digital audience.

7.5 Maximizing Engagement Through Data

Using data insights to boost engagement across social media channels is a pivotal strategy for entrepreneurs, marketing professionals, and social media managers aiming to elevate their brand presence. By leveraging analytics, businesses can tailor their content, optimize posting times, vary content formats, and understand competitors' strategies, all of which culminate in improved engagement and brand loyalty.

First, personalizing content tailoring is crucial. In today's diverse digital landscape, not all audiences respond equally to the same message. By harnessing data insights, businesses can segment their audience based on demographics, preferences, and behavior, ensuring that the messages resonate more deeply with each group. For instance, a brand targeting both millennials and baby boomers might use lighthearted memes for the former while opting for more straightforward, informative content for the latter. This targeted approach not only boosts interaction rates but also strengthens customer loyalty, as audiences feel that the content speaks directly to them.

Timing and frequency optimization is another key factor in maximizing social media engagement. Data analytics can reveal when an audience is most active on different platforms, allowing brands to schedule posts during peak times. For example, if a brand discovers through analytics that its audience is most active on Instagram around 7 p.m., it would be strategic to post content consistently at this time to maximize reach and interactions. Similarly, understanding the frequency of posts through analytical tools ensures that the brand remains visible without overwhelming its followers. Effective timing and frequency not only enhance engagement but also improve visibility and recall, leading to higher conversion rates over time.

Content variation plays a significant role in maintaining audience interest and catering to various user preferences. Different people are attracted to different forms of content – some may prefer videos, others infographics, or interactive polls. By experimenting with a blend of formats, brands can appeal to a broader audience and keep existing followers engaged. For example, a brand could use video tutorials to demonstrate product usage, infographics for statistics, or live Q&A sessions to foster real-time interaction. This diversity keeps the content fresh and prevents it from becoming monotonous, which is crucial in retaining audience attention and encouraging consistent engagement over time.

Monitoring competitors' strategies provides valuable insights into industry trends and potential areas for differentiation. By analyzing what competitors are doing well and identifying gaps they might be missing, businesses can refine their own strategies. For instance, if a competitor's Instagram stories featuring behind-the-scenes content receive high engagement, it might indicate a shared audience preference for transparency and authenticity. Adopting similar tactics, while adding unique elements, can help brands align better with audience expectations and differentiate themselves within the market. Moreover, understanding how competitors address customer queries and complaints can inform and improve social customer service strategies.

Social media competitor analysis tools are invaluable in conducting this monitoring, offering features such as tracking competitors' most engaging content, analyzing audience reactions, and identifying trending topics. These tools can show what types of content outperform others, providing a blueprint for success. For brands aiming to stand out, adopting successful tactics observed in competitors while distinguishing their uniqueness can guide productive adjustments to their content strategies and overall marketing approaches.

In summary, utilizing data insights for social media engagement involves a comprehensive approach that includes personalized content, optimal timing and frequency, varied content formats, and competitor analysis. Each of these components feeds into a strategy that not only increases engagement but also enhances customer satisfaction and brand loyalty. The focus on data-driven decisions ensures that content strategies are constantly evolving to meet changing consumer needs and preferences, ultimately driving sales and achieving business goals.

7.6 Final Thoughts

In this chapter, we've explored the integral role that analytics tools play in measuring and optimizing social media marketing efforts. Key performance indicators (KPIs) like Engagement Rate, Conversion Rate, Reach and Impressions, and Follower Growth Rate offer insights essential for crafting strategies that drive sales and enhance audience interaction. Understanding how these metrics connect allows entrepreneurs, marketing professionals, and social media managers to create data-driven approaches that align with their objectives. By focusing on analytics, businesses can refine their content, ensure a higher engagement rate, and adapt more swiftly to changing digital landscapes.

Beyond understanding individual KPIs, it's crucial to decode social media analytics by interpreting data within a broader context. Embracing data-driven decision-making through methods like A/B testing or using feedback loops equips businesses to improve strategies consistently. Furthermore, integrating analytics tools effectively into existing systems helps harness comprehensive insights, highlighting both immediate actions to take and long-term trends to consider. For those responsible for brand growth on social media, this chapter underscores the importance of aligning analytics with business goals, ensuring that social media efforts are not only effective but sustainable in driving engagement and boosting sales over time.

Chapter 8: Exploring Advanced Marketing Techniques

E xploring advanced marketing techniques is vital for any brand looking to enhance its digital presence and increase engagement. In today's fast-paced world, where technology continuously evolves, leveraging cutting-edge strategies can set a business apart from its competition. This chapter delves into how these innovative approaches can significantly impact marketing outcomes, especially when applied to social media platforms. By integrating advanced techniques into existing strategies, businesses can not only reach broader audiences but also cultivate stronger relationships with their current customers.

This chapter will explore several key areas where marketers can maximize the effectiveness of their social media efforts. It will cover the implementation of SEO strategies tailored specifically for social media to improve visibility and engagement. You'll learn about the seamless integration of email marketing with social media campaigns, which can amplify audience reach and drive higher conversions. Additionally, the chapter will discuss innovative content distribution channels that offer new opportunities for brand exposure and customer interaction.

Finally, it highlights cross-promotion techniques, illustrating ways to create a cohesive experience across all marketing channels. With analytics and optimization as underlying themes, this chapter provides actionable insights designed to help entrepreneurs, small business owners, and marketing professionals refine their social media tactics and stay ahead in the competitive digital landscape.

8.1 SEO Strategies for Social Media

Enhancing visibility and engagement on social media is a crucial strategy for entrepreneurs, marketers, and social media managers alike. One of the foundational techniques for achieving this is through keyword optimization in posts and profiles to improve discoverability. Keywords serve as the bridge between what users are searching for and the content that matches those queries. Integrating popular keywords into your social media content increases its chances of being displayed prominently in search results within social platforms. To identify the most effective keywords, it's advisable to leverage tools like Answer the Public or TikTok's Keyword Insights, which offer insights into popular search terms. The key is to use these terms naturally in your captions and descriptions without excessive repetition, as keyword stuffing can deter both algorithms and audiences.

Another effective method is implementing a strategic hashtag strategy by balancing popular and niche hashtags. Hashtags categorize content, making it easier for users interested in specific topics to find relevant posts. Utilizing a mix of both broad and specific hashtags allows you to reach a wider audience while targeting niche communities. For example, if you're posting about digital marketing, using a combination of #DigitalMarketing and #SmallBizSEO can attract diverse groups seeking general information or specialized advice. Tools like Buffer's hashtag manager can assist in organizing and storing these hashtags efficiently, ensuring consistency across posts.

Profile optimization is another key aspect, where having clear descriptions and consistent branding can markedly improve user engagement. Ensure that social media profiles represent your brand's voice and values succinctly. Descriptions should be informative yet concise, incorporating main keywords to enhance searchability. Also, maintaining visual consistency through profile pictures, cover images, and color schemes establishes a recognizable brand image. This not only aids in discoverability but also builds trust with potential followers.

Creating SEO-friendly content using engaging visuals and user-friendly layouts plays a significant role in capturing the audience's attention. Visual content like images and videos often engages more than plain text, so integrating eye-catching graphics can significantly boost interaction rates. Including alt-text for images enhances accessibility and can further improve SEO by providing additional context for search engines and visually impaired users.

In crafting such content, it's essential to focus on readability and layout. Ensuring that text is easily digestible with headings, bullet points, or short paragraphs can greatly affect how your content is perceived and shared. Keeping abreast of current trends—whether it's leveraging trending audio clips on TikTok or participating in meme culture—can enhance content relevance and encourage sharing among users, thus amplifying visibility.

Taking advantage of trending topics within your niche offers an opportunity to create timely and engaging content. By monitoring industry news and popular themes, you can align your posts with ongoing conversations, thereby attracting more interactions. For instance, marketers who rapidly align their posts with trending holidays or global events can see immediate spikes in engagement. This type of content capitalizes on the ephemeral nature of social media, keeping your brand dynamic and relevant.

Furthermore, tailoring strategies to the nuances of each social platform is vital. Each platform has unique characteristics and audience behaviors. On LinkedIn, professional language and industry-specific jargon might resonate well, whereas, on Instagram, a more casual tone with vibrant imagery may be more effective. Tailoring your approach ensures that your content aligns with user expectations on different platforms, increasing both engagement and the effectiveness of your messaging strategy.

A practical measure for sustaining long-term engagement is continually analyzing performance metrics. Tracking which types of posts garner the most views, likes, or shares can provide invaluable data on what your audience finds compelling. Regular analysis helps refine your strategy over time, enabling you to replicate successful tactics and discard less effective ones.

Additionally, fostering community engagement through interactive content such as polls, quizzes, or comment prompts encourages users to participate actively rather than passively consume content. This not only boosts engagement rates but also fosters a sense of community and connection between a brand and its followers. Social media platforms prioritize content that generates high levels of interaction, which, in turn, enhances visibility.

To tie all these strategies together, collaboration and consistency across all social media efforts are paramount. Collaborating with influencers or brands with complementary audiences can amplify reach and exposure. Such partnerships often introduce your content to new segments, diversifying your follower base and increasing overall engagement.

8.2 Integrating Email Marketing with Social Media

To effectively leverage the synergy between email and social media marketing, it is essential to understand how these two platforms can work together to enhance audience engagement. By integrating these channels strategically, marketers can amplify their reach, foster deeper connections with their audience, and ultimately drive higher conversions.

One effective method to promote email subscriptions using social media is by creating engaging posts that include clear calls-to-action (CTAs). These CTAs should direct followers to sign up for newsletters or special offers via email lists. Using social media profiles to highlight these incentives, such as exclusive discounts or early access to content, can encourage more users to subscribe. For instance, a fitness brand might post engaging workout tips on Instagram, inviting followers to join their email list for detailed plans or personalized advice.

Segmenting audiences based on insights gathered from social media interactions allows for more personalized communication through email campaigns. Social media analytics provide valuable data about user interests, behaviors, and demographics, which can be used to tailor email content. For example, if a brand notices that its Facebook audience frequently engages with sustainability-focused content, it can create specialized emails targeting environmentally-conscious products or initiatives. This approach ensures that the messaging resonates with specific segments, increasing the likelihood of engagement and conversion.

Repurposing successful social media content into email campaigns is another strategy that can enhance click rates. By taking high-performing posts—such as popular blog articles, videos, or customer testimonials—from social media and adapting them for email, marketers can maintain consistent messaging while extending the content's lifespan. This tactic not only reinforces key brand messages but also attracts email subscribers who may have missed the original posts. For instance, a popular Instagram post showcasing a new product could be transformed into an in-depth email feature, providing additional details and driving traffic back to the website.

Monitoring analytics is crucial for refining strategies and

optimizing content delivery across platforms. By regularly assessing metrics like open rates, click-through rates, and social media engagement, marketers can identify which tactics are most effective and make data-driven decisions to improve their campaigns. Tools that integrate analytics from both email and social media channels enable a comprehensive view of performance, facilitating adjustments to mail frequency, content style, or posting schedules. An ongoing focus on analysis ensures that marketing efforts remain agile and responsive to audience behaviors.

To create an integrated email and social media strategy, cross-promotion techniques are invaluable. Brands should ensure that email newsletters prominently feature CTAs encouraging subscribers to engage with their social media accounts. Similarly, social media posts should incentivize followers to join email lists, thus fostering a continuous cycle of audience growth and interaction. Hosting contests or giveaways on social media that require email sign-ups is a tangible way to increase email subscribers and boost engagement simultaneously.

Furthermore, segmentation strategies should be employed to enhance personalization in communications. By categorizing audiences based on data from social media interactions—such as engagement levels, viewed content, or shared interests—marketers can craft highly targeted email campaigns that speak directly to each group's preferences. Personalized emails show significantly higher engagement and conversion rates, making segmentation a vital component of any integrated marketing strategy.

Content repurposing remains a strategic advantage, allowing marketers to maximize the impact of their creations without constantly developing new material. By identifying top-performing social media content, brands can adapt it for email use, ensuring continuity in messaging while reaching different audience segments. A blog post that performed well on LinkedIn could serve as the basis for a series of informative emails, expanding on topics discussed in the original piece.

Lastly, analytics and tracking provide the foundation for on-going improvement in marketing strategies. By leveraging tools that aggregate data from both email and social media, marketers gain a holistic understanding of their audience's journey. Analyzing this data helps pinpoint areas that work well and those needing recalibration, enabling continuous enhancement of marketing tactics. Regular evaluation of success metrics facilitates informed decision-making and resource allocation, ultimately driving better outcomes for both email and social media channels.

8.3 Innovative Content Distribution Channels

In today's rapidly evolving digital landscape, expanding your reach through new content distribution channels is crucial for maximizing the effectiveness of social media marketing. This subpoint delves into innovative strategies that entrepreneurs, small business owners, and marketing professionals can adopt to enhance their brand presence and engage with wider audiences.

Engaging with emerging social media platforms is an essential strategy in staying ahead of trends and capturing new audiences. While mainstream platforms like Facebook and Instagram have dominated the social media space for years, emerging networks such as TikTok, Clubhouse, and BeReal offer unique opportunities for early adopters to connect with niche communities. By understanding the specific culture and user behavior on these platforms, businesses can tailor their content to resonate well with potential followers. For instance, TikTok's algorithm prioritizes authenticity and creativity, allowing brands to experiment with quirky and engaging content that might not perform as well on more established platforms. Investing time in exploring these new spaces can provide a first-mover advantage, offering an opportunity to build a strong community before the platform becomes saturated.

Non-traditional content formats like audio and video are powerful tools for fostering diverse engagement. With the surge in podcast consumption and video content across social media, businesses have the chance to reach audiences through multiple senses. Podcasts offer a personal touch, allowing brands to share insights, stories, and expert advice in a con- versational manner. Video content, especially short-form videos, has proven highly effective for viral marketing, given its shareability and entertainment value. Utilizing AI-driven tools to automate video creation can save marketers time while maintaining high-quality content, enhancing engagement with captivating visuals and dynamic storytelling.

Collaboration with brands or influencers is another effective way to expand reach by tapping into established audiences.

Partnering with influencers who align with your brand values amplifies your message and builds credibility among your target demographics. Influencers can seamlessly incorporate your product or service into their content, showcasing it authentically to their followers. Similarly, co-branding with other companies allows you to leverage each other's strengths and access new customer bases. These partnerships can include joint campaigns, contests, or giveaways, where both parties benefit from shared exposure. Collaborations foster a sense of community, encouraging cross-promotion that attracts followers from all involved parties.

Exploring unconventional promotional methods like virtual reality (VR) and gamification introduces exciting possibilities for creating memorable brand experiences. VR provides immersive environments where users can interact with products virtually, offering a futuristic shopping experience. It allows customers to visualize products in real-life scenarios, increasing confidence in purchase decisions. Gamification, on the other hand, involves integrating game-like elements into marketing strategies to boost user engagement. Challenges, rewards, and leaderboards make interactions more fun and competitive, encouraging users to participate actively. Both VR and gamification foster deeper engagement by delivering personalized ad experiences and gathering valuable data on user preferences and behavior. These innovative approaches keep users entertained while enhancing brand recall, driving organic growth as satisfied audiences share their experiences.

Guidelines to implement these strategies effectively start with thorough market research to understand which emerging platforms resonate with your audience. It's important to experiment with diverse content formats, measuring performance metrics to determine what works best. When collaborating with influencers or brands, ensure alignment in goals and values to maintain authenticity. Lastly, when adopting VR or gamification, personalize the experience to match user expectations for maximum impact.

8.4 Cross-Promotion Techniques

In today's dynamic marketing landscape, leveraging a coordinated use of channels is critical for maximizing the effectiveness of social media marketing strategies. With an abundance of digital tools at our fingertips, understanding how to integrate these channels can significantly enhance a brand's reach and engagement. One of the key tactics in this approach involves using social media as a gateway to drive traffic to other marketing channels and vice versa.

Social media platforms such as Facebook, Instagram, and LinkedIn offer brands the opportunity to engage directly with their audience through compelling content. The primary purpose here is to act as a catalyst that guides users toward additional marketing avenues like company websites, email newsletters, or even physical stores. By strategically placing links and calls-to-action within posts or bio sections, businesses can encourage users to explore further, thus extending their journey beyond the confines of social media. For instance, a well-timed Instagram Story can lead audiences to a blog post that delves deeper into a topic, thereby providing value while promoting other content hubs.

Just as social media drives users to other outlets, so too must those outlets push traffic back towards social media. This cyclical traffic flow not only maximizes audience interaction but also maintains brand visibility across multiple platforms. Businesses can embed social media feeds on their websites or include them in email campaigns, offering seamless pathways for users to follow updates and engage with real-time content. This reciprocal relationship between channels ensures that each platform enhances the other's impact, ultimately fostering stronger customer relations and loyalty.

Another essential element in this strategy is maintaining cohesive messaging across all channels to ensure brand consistency. Today's consumers expect a unified experience regardless of the touchpoint. Consistency isn't just about visual identity— like logos and color schemes—but extends to the tone and voice of the communication. Creating cohesive messages involves crafting narratives that reflect a brand's values and core offerings, serialized across different formats to reinforce the brand story.

Take, for example, a new product launch. The message communicated should be consistent whether it's through a tweet, a video advertisement, or a press release. This coherence assures customers that they are interacting with the same entity, building trust and recognition. Tools such as editorial calendars and style guides can help marketers plan and audit their communications effectively, thus ensuring uniformity and clarity.

To entice cross-platform engagement, employing targeted

offers and exclusive content is particularly potent. Exclusive deals or sneak peeks available only through specific channels can drive audience interest and increase participation. For instance, offering a discount code via a newsletter that can be redeemed only when followers engage with a particular Tweet encourages traffic between email and social media, enhancing interaction rates. Similarly, exclusive behind-the-scenes content posted on a single channel invites users from other platforms to join, broadening engagement.

Such strategic incentives don't just amplify audience numbers but deepen customer involvement, leading to increased brand advocacy. Personalizing content for different segments based on platform demographics or user behavior can make offers more attractive and relevant, thereby maximizing conversion opportunities. By tailoring content and incentives to fit the unique culture of each platform, businesses ensure that their messages resonate more deeply with their audience, increasing the likelihood of successful conversions.

A critical aspect of this integrated strategy involves evaluating performance metrics to assess the success of cross-promotion efforts. Critical Key Performance Indicators (KPIs) such as click-through rates, conversion rates, engagement levels, and return on investment (ROI) provide valuable insights into how effective these strategies are. Social media analytics tools track user interactions and can pinpoint which pieces of content are driving the most traffic or engagements.

Regularly monitoring these metrics allows businesses to make data-driven decisions, optimally allocate resources, and refine their marketing strategies to better align with audience preferences. Are certain channels underperforming compared to others? If so, organizations may need to revisit their content placement and audience targeting strategies. A/B testing can also reveal which types of content or offers work best across different demographics, enabling marketers to continuously optimize their approaches.

Beyond traditional metrics, qualitative assessments like customer feedback or sentiment analysis can reveal deeper insights into consumer perceptions and experiences. By combining quantitative data with these qualitative insights, businesses can fine-tune their cross-channel strategies to not only meet business objectives but also enhance overall customer satisfaction.

8.5 Analytics and Optimization

To improve marketing tactics through data-driven insights, it's crucial to regularly analyze engagement data. This practice helps marketers understand audience behavior, preferences, and trends over time, providing a solid foundation for tailoring marketing strategies. For instance, by examining data on user interactions, marketers can identify the types of content that resonate most with their audience, be it videos, infographics, or blog posts. Understanding these preferences allows businesses to curate more relevant and appealing content, ultimately boosting engagement and fostering stronger connections with their audience.

Furthermore, analyzing engagement data helps pinpoint peak

usage times when the target audience is most active online. By scheduling posts and marketing campaigns during these periods, businesses can enhance visibility and ensure that messages reach the audience at optimal times. This targeted approach not only increases engagement but also maximizes the return on investment for marketing efforts.

Conducting A/B testing is another essential tactic for optimizing content presentation and delivery. A/B testing involves comparing two versions of a campaign or piece of content to determine which performs better. For example, a business might test different headlines, images, or calls-to-action on its website to see which version drives higher click-through rates or conversions. Through A/B testing, marketers gain valuable insights into what elements are most effective in catching the audience's attention and encouraging them to take desired actions.

A key component of A/B testing is setting clear objectives and selecting relevant metrics to measure success. These objectives should align with overall marketing goals, such as increasing conversion rates or enhancing user engagement. By establishing specific criteria for success, marketers can accurately evaluate the impact of their tests and make informed decisions about future strategies.

Integrating metrics from multiple platforms provides a comprehensive view of marketing performance. In today's digital landscape, businesses often utilize various channels to reach their audience, including social media, email marketing, and websites. By aggregating data from these sources, marketers can obtain a holistic understanding of how different channels contribute to overall marketing success. This integration enables businesses to identify which channels are most effective in reaching their target audience and tailor their strategies accordingly.

Moreover, integrating data across platforms allows for more accurate tracking of user journeys, helping marketers understand how customers interact with their brand across different touchpoints. This insight is invaluable in creating seamless and consistent customer experiences, ensuring that messages are aligned and reinforce the brand's value proposition.

Identifying areas of improvement is crucial for strategically adjusting marketing plans. By regularly evaluating marketing metrics, businesses can spot trends and patterns that indicate where changes are needed. For instance, if a particular piece of content consistently underperforms, it may suggest that the message isn't resonating with the audience or that the format needs adjustment. Addressing these issues ensures that marketing efforts remain effective and responsive to changing consumer preferences.

Another area that benefits from ongoing analysis is the identification of common drop-off points, where users disengage from the brand. These drop-offs can occur at various stages of the customer journey, from initial interest to final purchase. By understanding where and why these drop-offs happen, marketers can implement targeted re-engagement strategies and optimize user experiences to reduce churn and increase conversions.

Data-driven insights empower businesses to adopt a proactive approach to marketing, allowing them to anticipate challenges and adjust strategies dynamically. This agility is particularly vital in today's fast-paced digital market, where consumer preferences and technological advancements evolve rapidly.

In addition to leveraging quantitative data, incorporating qualitative insights from user feedback and surveys can enrich the understanding of audience behavior. Qualitative data provides context and depth to quantitative findings, revealing the underlying motivations and needs driving consumer actions. By combining these insights, marketers can craft more personalized and compelling marketing messages that truly resonate with their target audience.

8.6 Final Thoughts

In this chapter, we have delved into maximizing social media marketing effectiveness by integrating SEO, email strategies, and innovative content distribution. By optimizing keywords, using strategic hashtags, and enhancing profiles, businesses can increase the discoverability and engagement of their social media content. These methods help ensure that your brand's voice is consistent and recognizable across various platforms. Furthermore, integrating email marketing with social media allows for a cohesive strategy that nurtures deeper connections with audiences through personalized communication and cross-promotion techniques. Effective use of data analytics helps refine these tactics to sustain engagement and improve overall performance.

Additionally, exploring new channels and formats is essential in today's ever-changing digital landscape. Engaging with emerging platforms and experimenting with formats like audio and video enables businesses to expand their reach and capture diverse audience groups. Collaborations with influencers and brands can amplify messaging and foster community growth, while innovative approaches like virtual reality and gamification offer unique ways to engage users. Throughout, maintaining consistency across all channels ensures a unified brand experience, reinforcing trust and encouraging loyalty from your audience. By combining these strategies with regular analysis and optimization, marketers can adapt to trends and drive sustained success in social media marketing.

Chapter 9: Staying Ahead of Social Media Trends

S taying ahead of social media trends is essential for anyone looking to maintain a strong presence in the digital landscape. In an age where social media platforms continuously evolve, understanding and adapting to these changes can mean the difference between leading the market or lagging behind. Social media is not just a tool for connection; it's a dynamic environment where trends emerge rapidly, influencing consumer behavior. As such, staying current with what's trending allows businesses and marketing professionals to make informed decisions that keep them relevant and competitive. This chapter will guide you through the intricacies of spotting these emerging trends effectively.

In this chapter, readers will learn the value of identifying new trends before they become widespread. The text provides strategies for using industry reports to decipher market movements and understand consumer behavior patterns. An emphasis is placed on data-driven decision-making as a crucial part of trend identification, reducing reliance on assumptions and ensuring alignment with business goals. The chapter explores the benefits of social listening tools to track audience interests and the role of influencers and industry conferences in staying knowledgeable about what's to come. Furthermore, it explains how to evaluate trends for relevance to a brand's niche and the significance of observing competitor moves to find opportunities for differentiation. Through these discussions, the chapter aims to equip entrepreneurs, marketing professionals, and social media managers with practical insights needed to navigate the ever-changing social media world successfully.

9.1 Identifying Emerging Social Media Trends

Spotting new trends before they become mainstream is an invaluable skill for entrepreneurs, marketing professionals, and social media managers seeking to stay ahead of the curve. By identifying emerging trends early, brands can position themselves as industry leaders, rather than followers, capturing the attention of their audience while competitors are still catching up.

One of the most effective ways to uncover upcoming trends is by monitoring industry reports. These reports often contain detailed analyses of market movements and consumer behavior patterns. They provide insights into shifts in the industry landscape, and understanding these shifts allows businesses to anticipate changes and adapt their strategies proactively. For example, fashion industries may notice a surge in sustainable fashion based on trends highlighted in such reports, enabling them to incorporate eco-friendly materials into their product lines before the trend becomes widespread.

To leverage these industry reports effectively, it's crucial to make data-driven decisions. Rather than reacting impulsively to every apparent trend, analyzing data helps determine which trends hold genuine promise and align with business goals. Utilizing data from reports ensures that decisions are based on evidence rather than assumptions, reducing the risk of following fads that may not resonate with the target audience. This approach aids in resource allocation, ensuring that investment is funneled toward trends that offer real potential for growth.

Another powerful tool for spotting trends is engaging in trend-driven content creation. When brands capitalize on emerging trends through relevant content, they not only capture audience interest but also establish themselves as thought leaders. Trend-driven content is relatable and timely, making it more likely to be shared and engaged with, thus amplifying the brand's reach. A case in point is how some beverage brands embraced the Dalgona coffee trend during the pandemic, creating their own unique versions to engage their audience and boost visibility.

Social listening tools are invaluable for providing insights into audience interests and curating relevant content. These tools allow brands to track conversations and sentiments online, offering a window into what topics and themes are gaining traction among audiences. With social listening, brands can identify subtle shifts in consumer preferences and respond accordingly. For instance, if a significant number of users express interest in virtual experiences, a travel company might explore virtual tours as part of their offerings.

Monitoring industry reports and leveraging social listening

tools go hand in hand. While reports offer broader scope data and long-term trends, social listening provides immediate feedback on consumer sentiment and engagement with current happenings. This combination is potent for brands aiming to craft content that resonates strongly with their audience.

Another aspect to consider when adopting new trends is relevance to your niche. Jumping on every trend can dilute a brand's focus and confuse audiences about its core message. It's essential to evaluate whether a trend aligns with the brand's identity and values. Narrowing down to trends relevant to your niche ensures that efforts are concentrated on areas that genuinely enhance brand positioning and engagement. For example, during the pandemic, Tourism Ireland leveraged the #armchairtravel hashtag because it aligned with their core offering – exploring destinations virtually during restrictions. This ensured both relevance and increased engagement from home-bound audiences invited to experience Irish locations digitally.

Inclusion of influencers in your trend-spotting strategy can also yield significant benefits. Influencers often have their finger on the pulse of what's emerging, sometimes even setting trends themselves. Engaging with industry influencers not only keeps you updated about the latest trends but also creates opportunities for collaboration to amplify your brand's message further. Commenting on influencer posts and involving them in your campaigns can help tap into their networks, reaching wider audiences interested in fresh perspectives.

Additionally, attending industry conferences and trade shows can serve as a goldmine for trend-spotting. Conference discussions, keynote speeches, and networking opportunities provide firsthand insights into what's new and buzzing in various sectors. Such events highlight innovative projects or technologies that might soon become mainstream, offering businesses a competitive advantage by preparing them to act early.

Keeping an eye on competitor moves also assists in recognizing worthwhile trends. If competitors are starting to engage with a particular trend, it's worth examining why and how they're approaching it. However, it's not just about copying others; it's about understanding the strategic fit and distinctive application for your brand. Benchmarking performance metrics against competitors can reveal gaps and opportunities for differentiation that align with your company's strengths and market position.

Ultimately, identifying and adopting new trends should align with your strategic goals. The alignment ensures that these trends support broader business objectives and contribute meaningfully to the brand's long-term vision. Before jumping on any trend, it's important to conduct a strategic review to see if it complements the brand's missions and contributes positively towards achieving set goals.

9.2 Experimenting with New Features

In the ever-evolving landscape of social media marketing, staying ahead of trends and features is critical for brands seeking differentiation and market leadership. One effective strategy for achieving this is embracing new platform features as soon as they become available. Testing these features upon their launch can not only lead to exceptional engagement opportunities but also ensures that a brand stands out from its competitors.

When a social media platform introduces a new feature, it often creates a wave of curiosity and excitement among users. By being one of the first to experiment with this feature, brands can capture audience attention more effectively than those who wait. For instance, when Instagram introduced Stories, early adopters leveraged the visual storytelling potential to enhance engagement with their audience. These brands gained an advantage by offering content in a format that was fresh and exciting at the time. Similarly, exploring the functionality of newly launched features like Lemon8's templates or TikTok's duet option can unveil creative ways to interact with audiences, fostering deeper connections and increasing engagement before others catch on.

Early adoption offers significant benefits beyond just initial user engagement. It enhances a brand's visibility and reach by positioning it as an innovator. Platforms often promote content using their new features to encourage widespread use. This preferential treatment can lead to increased exposure and higher ranking in user feeds. Brands that seize these opportunities often find themselves at the forefront of trending topics, gaining organic traction and amplifying their message without additional cost. For instance, businesses that quickly adapted to Facebook Live saw substantial growth in reach and interaction, simply because they embraced the live streaming feature while it was still new.

Feedback obtained during the experimentation phase is in-valuable for refining broader marketing strategies. By testing different approaches with new features, brands can gather insights into what resonates with their audience and optimize their content accordingly. For example, a company might experiment with Polls within Instagram Stories to gauge cus-tomer preferences, which can then inform product develop-ment or marketing campaigns. This iterative process allows brands to craft messages that are more closely aligned with audience interests, paving the way for successful broader applications.

Moreover, this feedback loop provides empirical data that can be used to make informed decisions across other channels or platforms. Analyzing performance metrics collected from early feature tests aids in recognizing patterns and identifying tactics that effectively boost engagement. Through such analysis, brands can fine-tune their approach, ensuring that any future content is better targeted and more likely to yield positive results.

Experimentation with new features also paves the way for discovering innovative content solutions that can enhance customer loyalty. By continuously exploring and adapting to new tools, brands remain dynamic and relevant. This adaptability demonstrates a commitment to providing value and keeping pace with industry developments, which resonates well with customers. For example, brands that integrated aug-mented reality filters into their Snapchat campaigns provided interactive experiences that delighted users, fostering brand affinity and loyalty.

Furthermore, experimenting with unique content formats can set a brand apart as a leader in creativity and innovation. Audiences appreciate brands that are willing to push boundaries and offer fresh, engaging experiences. Innovation in content, whether through gamification, personalized interactions, or immersive storytelling, keeps the audience intrigued and encourages repeat engagement. Such a strategy not only maintains current customer interest but attracts new followers intrigued by the novel content offerings.

However, successful early adoption requires a strategic mindset and proper resource allocation. Brands need to have teams ready to jump on new features, conduct trials, and analyze outcomes swiftly. Maintaining an agile marketing strategy enables quick pivots based on real-time data. Monitoring industry trends, competitor movements, and platform announcements ensures brands are prepared to capitalize on emerging opportunities promptly.

The importance of integration and collaboration cannot be overstated in this context. Cross-functional teams working together—from marketing to IT—ensure a seamless execution of experiments and implementation of insights. Collaboration with influencers or thought leaders can also amplify early adoption efforts, lending credibility and expanding reach through established networks. Engaging influencers familiar with the new feature can provide authentic demonstrations, further enticing target audiences.

As the dynamics of social media continue to shift rapidly, marketers must remain vigilant and proactive in their approach. Experimenting with new features is not merely a tactic for immediate gains; it is a long-term strategy for building a robust, adaptable brand presence. By taking calculated risks and embracing change, businesses position themselves at the forefront of industry transformation, securing a competitive edge that supports sustained growth and market relevance.

9.3 Adapting to Platform Algorithm Changes

Staying agile amidst changing social media algorithms is a continuous process that requires active participation and adaptation from businesses and marketers. The rapidly shifting landscape of social media means algorithms are frequently updated, affecting how content gets distributed, ranked, and discovered by users. It is crucial for entrepreneurs, small business owners, marketing professionals, and social media managers to stay informed about these changes to maintain engagement and reach. Understanding the nature of these updates allows businesses to anticipate potential changes, thereby reducing strategy disruptions.

One of the fundamental strategies for staying ahead in this dynamic environment is regularly reviewing platform updates. Social media platforms such as Facebook, Instagram, LinkedIn, and Twitter frequently refine their algorithms to improve user experience and engagement. These updates often influence which types of content are favored, impacting visibility and reach. By actively monitoring official announcements and algorithm reports, businesses can prepare in advance to tweak their strategies accordingly, ensuring minimal disruption when the changes take effect. This proactive approach helps maintain a stable presence on social media platforms, keeping audiences engaged.

To further cushion against the impacts of algorithm shifts, developing versatile content strategies is vital. Diverse content approaches ensure that regardless of how an algorithm changes, there is always a way to engage with audiences constructively. For instance, combining short-form videos, infographics, compelling text posts, and engaging interactive elements like polls can cover a wide range of user preferences. A varied content strategy not only caters to different user tastes but also maximizes opportunities for engagement across multiple touchpoints. Consistency in posting diversified content keeps the audience interested and aids in bypassing any adverse effects due to changes in algorithmic priorities.

Community discussions offer another layer of insight for navigating algorithm changes. Engaging in conversations within industry networks or social media forums brings together experts who share firsthand experiences and strategic pivots related to new algorithm developments. These discussions allow participants to exchange ideas, learn from others' successes or mistakes, and formulate smarter responses to ongoing changes. By integrating shared knowledge into one's own strategies, brands can adapt more effectively, using real-time insights to guide decision-making processes.

Moreover, analyzing competitor strategies serves as an invaluable tactic to unveil new methods for adapting to evolving algorithms. Observing how competitors respond to similar challenges provides a benchmark for assessing one's own strategies and discovering innovative approaches. When a brand successfully navigates an algorithm update, adopting some of its tactics might help other businesses achieve similar success. This practice not only speeds up the learning curve but also inspires fresh ideas tailored to maintaining relevance and competitive advantage. Competitive analysis encourages innovation, prompting businesses to go beyond conventional methods and foster an inventive spirit within their teams.

Leveraging social listening tools enhances the ability to collect essential data about audience interactions and sentiments regarding various trends. These tools enable marketers to analyze the effectiveness of their content strategies and adjust them according to prevailing audience preferences. Having access to accurate analytics supports informed decision-making, helping brands deliver relevant content aligned with algorithmic trends. Social listening tools also allow businesses to track mentions, identify influencers, and monitor brand sentiment. By understanding how target audiences interact with content, marketers can make strategic adjustments more swiftly and efficiently.

Understanding algorithm nuances across different platforms leads to tailored strategies rather than a generic approach. Each platform has specific ranking factors such as engagement rates, recency, and content relevance. For example, LinkedIn prioritizes professional content engagement, while Instagram focuses heavily on visual storytelling through Reels and Stories. Recognizing these differences enables marketers to tailor their content style and timing to match each platform's preferences.

9.4 Participating in Industry Communities

Engaging in communities is vital for entrepreneurs, marketing professionals, and social media managers who wish to stay ahead of social media trends. It involves leveraging the power of collaboration and knowledge-sharing within relevant social media groups, which are abundant with practical insights that can help one remain competitive in this fast-paced digital landscape.

One of the most effective ways to tap into community learning is by joining social media groups related to your industry or area of interest. These groups serve as hubs for like-minded individuals where members share experiences, strategies, and updates on the latest trends. Such platforms create an atmosphere of collaboration, enabling participants to exchange ideas and learn from each other's successes and challenges. This shared knowledge not only provides fresh perspectives but also helps in identifying emerging trends before they become widespread, giving you a competitive edge.

Participating in webinars and conferences is another strategic approach to staying informed about new trends and resources in social media marketing. These events are often led by industry experts and thought leaders who provide valuable insights into the evolving dynamics of social media platforms. Webinars offer interactive sessions where attendees can ask questions and engage directly with speakers, facilitating deeper understanding. Conferences, on the other hand, provide opportunities for networking and gaining firsthand information about upcoming tools and techniques that can enhance brand presence on social media. By attending such events regularly, participants remain at the forefront of industry developments.

In addition to informal sharing through groups and events, enrolling in structured online courses can offer comprehensive learning on emerging social media trends. Online courses are designed to provide detailed content tailored to specific marketing needs, allowing learners to gain actionable insights that can be directly applied to their business strategies. Many courses include modules on analytics, content creation, and platform-specific strategies, all of which are crucial for navigating the complexities of social media marketing. Completing these courses not only equips marketers with up-to-date knowledge but also showcases their commitment to continuous professional development.

Moreover, engaging in trend debates within communities plays a critical role in refining marketing strategies and establishing brands as thought leaders. Debate forums and discussion panels allow marketers to explore different viewpoints and understand the implications of various trends on their marketing efforts. These exchanges help clarify strategies and foster innovative thinking by challenging conventional methods. Brands that actively participate in these discussions position themselves as progressive and forward-thinking entities, which attracts attention and trust from their audience.

By collaborating in these communities, marketers also contribute to the evolution of best practices that can benefit wider audiences. Sharing discoveries, testing results, and campaign feedback not only enhances individual learning but also enriches the collective wisdom of the community. This cycle of knowledge-sharing accelerates innovation and reduces the learning curve for members, allowing them to implement effective strategies swiftly and efficiently.

To maximize the benefits of community engagement, it is essential to approach it strategically. Begin by identifying active and reputable groups that align with your marketing objectives. Engage consistently by participating in discussions, asking questions, and offering valuable insights. When attending webinars and conferences, focus on sessions that address current challenges and emerging opportunities in social media to ensure relevance to your business context. Additionally, choose online courses that offer certifications, as these credentials can add value to your professional profile.

The time invested in community engagement pays off significantly when it comes to maintaining a competitive advantage. In an era where algorithm changes and consumer behaviors shift rapidly, being part of a community provides timely access to information that could otherwise be missed. Social media is a dynamic field that rewards those who are proactive in seeking knowledge and adapting to changes swiftly.

9.5 Analyzing Competitor Strategies

In the fast-paced world of social media marketing, staying ahead requires a keen understanding of how competitors navigate the landscape. Utilizing competitor analysis is not just a beneficial practice; it is essential for discovering innovative approaches and ensuring continuous improvement in your strategies. By observing and learning from what others do well, as well as what they miss, businesses can position themselves to not only keep up with trends but also set them.

One of the primary benefits of closely analyzing competitors is gaining insights into engagement rates. Observing how companies engage their audience on social media can inform strategic adjustments. For instance, if a competitor sees a spike in interaction following a specific type of post or campaign, this suggests that similar content could work for your brand too. Alternatively, lower engagement might indicate what to avoid or improve upon. This approach allows you to be dynamic and responsive, shaping content and engagement strategies that are timely and relevant.

Learning from successful adaptations also plays a crucial role in refining your social media tactics. When competitors discover new methods or tools that resonantly connect with consumers, adopting similar strategies can accelerate your learning curve. It's about fostering a culture of improvement by seeing what works and then iterating upon it. This doesn't mean copying another brand's strategy note-for-note, but rather using their successes as a springboard to innovate further and customize these ideas to fit your unique brand voice and objectives.

Moreover, competitive analysis often unveils lesser-known strategies that maintain relevance and differentiation in crowded markets. Understanding not just what direct rivals are doing, but also indirect ones, can reveal opportunities to differentiate and stay relevant. This might involve exploring niche channels that competitors have overlooked or tapping into emerging technologies that offer a fresh way to connect with audiences. By employing these tactics, you ensure your brand continually stands out, even as market conditions evolve.

Continuous monitoring of competitors' actions helps uncover opportunities for strategic innovation. By keeping an eye on the broader competitive environment, you gain insights into industry shifts and consumer preferences, which can inform your long-term planning. For example, if you notice a trend among competitors towards more sustainable practices, you might explore implementing eco-friendly initiatives of your own, meeting a growing customer demand before it becomes mainstream. Such initiatives not only align with evolving consumer values but can also set you apart as a leader in sustainability within your industry.

Developing versatile content strategies also necessitates watching competitors closely. As algorithms change, so does the effectiveness of certain types of content. Having a diverse content strategy that includes videos, stories, and images can help shield against algorithm biases. If a competitor's video series consistently garners high engagement, analyzing why it's successful might help tailor your content to similar standards, ensuring consistent audience connection.

Engaging in community discussions related to your industry can provide additional layers of insight and networking opportunities. Participating in relevant forums, groups, or online courses involves listening to what others in your space are discussing, offering practical insights that complement what you learn from formal competitor analysis. These interactions allow you to validate your observations about competitor behavior, glean new ideas, and refine your strategies in real-time, reinforcing your brand's presence as informed and engaged in its community.

Leveraging online courses and workshops focused on social media trends keeps your skills sharp and up-to-date, ensuring you can apply learned strategies effectively. These educational resources often highlight case studies including competitor success stories, demonstrating practical applications of theory. They also emphasize emerging trends that prepare you to leverage new technologies and methodologies even before competitors do, culminating in a proactive approach to trend adoption and innovation.

Participating in trend debates also offers significant advantages in identifying new ways to differentiate your brand. During these discussions, thought leaders share insights that challenge traditional thinking and introduce novel concepts. Engaging in these debates not only informs you about future directions but also reinforces your brand's authority in social media marketing. By contributing to these dialogues, you position your business as forward-thinking, capable of setting trends rather than merely following them.

9.6 Final Thoughts

In today's fast-paced digital world, staying updated with the latest trends in social media marketing is essential for success. Throughout this chapter, we've explored various strategies that entrepreneurs, marketing professionals, and social media managers can employ to remain competitive. From utilizing industry reports for identifying emerging trends to leveraging social listening tools for immediate insights, the chapter emphasizes making data-driven decisions. By incorporating relevant trends into their branding efforts, businesses can effectively capture audience interest and establish themselves as leaders in their field. Engaging with influencers, attending conferences, and keenly observing competitor moves further enhance one's ability to spot and adapt to valuable trends, ensuring that resources are directed toward genuine growth opportunities.

The chapter also highlights the importance of experimenting with new platform features and adapting to changing algorithms, underscoring the need for agility in social media strategies. Embracing new features early on offers brands a chance to be at the forefront of innovation, while understanding algorithm changes helps maintain strong engagement and reach. Collaborating within industry communities provides a rich source of knowledge and fresh ideas, promoting continuous learning and improvement. Ultimately, by integrating these approaches, individuals and businesses can keep their social media presence dynamic and effective, driving customer engagement and reinforcing brand loyalty in an ever-evolving landscape.

Chapter 10: Case Studies and Real-World Applications

C ase studies and real-world applications offer valuable insights into the dynamics of successful brand campaigns in social media marketing. Examining these practical examples allows us to understand what makes certain campaigns stand out while others falter. By exploring renowned brand strategies, we can identify patterns that contribute to success and learn how to avoid common pitfalls. In this context, the study of various campaigns provides a roadmap for businesses aiming to enhance their social media presence.

This chapter delves into a range of successful campaigns, highlighting key elements such as emotional connection, personalization, user-generated content, and humor. It will analyze iconic campaigns like Nike's "Just Do It," Coca-Cola's "Share a Coke," Airbnb's endeavors, and Old Spice's humorous transformation. Each campaign showcases different aspects of effective branding, offering lessons on engaging consumers and building strong brand relationships. Additionally, the chapter addresses the importance of understanding cultural sensitivities and having strategies for crisis management.

Through these case studies, entrepreneurs, marketing professionals, and social media managers can extract valuable
lessons to apply to their own campaigns, ultimately improving
brand engagement and consumer loyalty.

10.1 Successful Brand Campaigns Analysis

In the realm of social media marketing, understanding what
transforms a campaign into a success is crucial for both emerging and established brands. By dissecting renowned campaigns,
we can uncover strategies that contributed to their effectiveness.

One exemplary campaign that set the standard in brand affinity
and emotional connection is Nike's "Just Do It." Launched
in 1988, this campaign tapped into the deeper motivations
of not just athletes but also everyday individuals striving to
achieve their best. The simplicity and universality of the slogan
resonated with a broad audience, creating a powerful emotional
bond. This emotional connection, coupled with consistent
messaging across various channels, reinforced Nike's core values and helped it maintain relevance over decades. This long-
standing campaign has significantly boosted Nike's market
presence and continues to be a pivotal element in its branding
strategy. The emotional ties formed by the campaign have
fostered consumer loyalty, making "Just Do It" synonymous
with personal empowerment and perseverance.

Another noteworthy campaign illustrating the power of personalization is Coca-Cola's "Share a Coke." Initiated in Australia
in 2011, this campaign involved replacing the iconic Coca-Cola

logo on bottles with common first names. This simple yet ingenious idea turned an ordinary product into something personal and shareable. By encouraging consumers to find bottles with their names and share photos on social media using the hashtag #ShareaCoke, Coca-Cola effectively engaged consumers on a personal level. This personalization strategy revitalized Coca-Cola's appeal among younger demographics, reversing sales declines and sparking significant social media interaction. By localizing the campaign to include popular names in different markets, Coca-Cola ensured widespread participation and engagement, which was key in driving its success.

Additionally, Airbnb's adept use of user-generated content exemplifies how community-driven stories can build trust and authenticity. Through initiatives like the "Belong Anywhere" campaign, Airbnb encouraged users to share their personal travel experiences on the platform. This approach not only enhanced the company's image as a community-focused service but also provided potential customers with relatable and trustworthy content. The strategy of leveraging real stories from diverse users helped reinforce Airbnb's commitment to inclusivity and global community-building. As highlighted in Source 1, Airbnb's ability to connect emotionally with its audience and showcase genuine experiences played a critical role in establishing its brand as more than just a rental service.

Lastly, Old Spice's transformation through humor and rapid-adaptation strategies demonstrates the impact of creative branding. The "The Man Your Man Could Smell Like" campaign used witty and memorable commercials to reposition

Old Spice from a dated brand to a contemporary favorite. This campaign broke traditional gender norms by targeting the advertisements at women who purchase grooming products for men, thus expanding their audience. The humor employed captured attention and went viral, generating countless online parodies and discussions. As Source 1 indicates, Old Spice's ability to rapidly adapt its messaging and create engaging content in real-time was instrumental in regaining market share and cementing its place in modern pop culture.

In analyzing these successful campaigns, several key strategies emerge. Nike and Coca-Cola demonstrate the significance of emotional and personal connections in building brand affinity and engaging consumers. Meanwhile, Airbnb and Old Spice highlight the value of user-generated content and humor in fostering authenticity and relatability. Each of these elements underscores the importance of understanding one's audience and crafting campaigns that resonate on a personal level.

For entrepreneurs and small business owners aiming to en-hance their social media presence, these insights offer valuable lessons. By aligning brand messages with audience values and emotions, businesses can forge stronger relationships with consumers, increasing loyalty and advocacy. Additionally, in-corporating personalization and encouraging user-generated content allow brands to engage customers directly, creating a sense of community and shared purpose.

For marketing professionals and social media managers, these case studies serve as benchmarks for implementing effective strategies. By studying what made these campaigns succeed, marketers can refine their own approaches, ensuring that their efforts resonate and achieve intended outcomes.

10.2 Lessons Learned from Failures

When examining the pitfalls of social media marketing, it is crucial to understand that failures can offer valuable cautionary lessons. One of the most notable examples is Pepsi's 2017 ad featuring Kendall Jenner. This campaign faced severe backlash due to its lack of cultural sensitivity and tone-deaf approach. Aiming to portray a message of unity, the advertisement showed Jenner offering a can of Pepsi to a police officer during a protest, which was perceived as an attempt to trivialize serious social justice issues, particularly the Black Lives Matter movement. The public outrage was immediate and widespread, highlighting the importance of understanding cultural contexts and audience sentiments when crafting marketing messages. This incident taught brands the necessity of authentic storytelling and respecting sociopolitical climates to avoid alienating their audience.

Another case study worth considering is McDonald's #McD-Stories campaign, which intended to leverage user-generated stories about positive experiences with the brand. However, this initiative quickly backfired as the hashtag became a hub for negative customer feedback and sarcastic remarks about McDonald's products and services. The swift transformation of a promotional effort into a PR nightmare underscores the need for comprehensive audience moderation and crisis management plans. In social media marketing, companies must be prepared to handle both expected and unexpected

SOCIAL MEDIA MARKETING SECRETS

responses from their audience. Planning for potential backlash and having strategies in place to manage such situations can help mitigate damage and turn negative situations into opportunities for improvement and engagement.

United Airlines provides another cautionary tale about the power of social media and the necessity of swift, transparent communication during crises. In 2017, a video of a passenger being forcibly removed from a flight went viral, causing a massive public relations disaster for the airline. The airline's initial response was criticized for lacking empathy and transparency, exacerbating the situation further. This incident demonstrates the critical role of timely and genuine communication in crisis management. Companies should prioritize open and honest dialogue, taking responsibility and showing willingness to address customer grievances effectively. This approach not only helps control the narrative but also rebuilds trust with the audience over time.

The case of Snapchat's gender bias incident illustrates the risks associated with assumptions in audience targeting and emphasizes the importance of inclusive messaging. When Snapchat launched a new filter that perpetuated stereotypical gender norms, it faced significant backlash from users who felt marginalized. This incident serves as a reminder that inclusivity should be at the forefront of campaign design. Marketers must prioritize diversity and representation to resonate with a broader audience and foster a sense of belonging among all users. In a diverse social landscape, assumptions can lead to unintended exclusions, damaging brand reputation and limiting market reach. Incorporating diverse perspectives and testing campaigns across various demographics can preemptively address these challenges and facilitate more effective, inclusive marketing efforts.

10.3 Adapting Case Study Strategies to Your Business

In the rapidly evolving world of social media marketing, learning how to apply insights gleaned from successful case studies can be a game-changer for businesses seeking to enhance their online presence and engagement. Entrepreneurs, marketing professionals, and social media managers alike can benefit from understanding how to tailor existing strategies to suit their unique circumstances. By dissecting what works in other contexts and morphing those elements to fit your brand, you can develop campaigns that resonate deeply with your audience.

Identifying relevant elements for your brand involves recognizing and tailoring strategies that strike a chord with your target demographic. This approach is not merely about replicating a tactic seen in a successful campaign but about understanding why it worked. For instance, if a particular branding element was effective due to its cultural relevance or emotional appeal, determine if similar themes align with your brand values and audience preferences.

User-generated content (UGC) offers an effective method to engage with your audience on a personal level. Encouraging customers to contribute through surveys or sharing their experiences can foster a sense of community around your brand. UGC not only provides authentic content but also enhances brand loyalty by making consumers feel like integral parts of a larger narrative. Surveying your audience or incentivizing them to share their stories can uncover rich insights into consumer preferences, offering material that marketing teams might not have imagined independently.

Additionally, analyzing competitors' failures is as critical as studying their successes. Every unsuccessful campaign holds lessons about what not to do. Understanding these missteps enables businesses to refine their strategies, avoid similar pitfalls, and craft more resilient campaigns. A careful review of where others have stumbled allows brands to swiftly adapt to market feedback, ensuring they remain agile and responsive to changing consumer sentiments.

Building agility into your marketing model is essential for navigating the fast-paced digital landscape. An agile approach emphasizes responsiveness and real-time engagement, turning potential challenges into opportunities for growth. This approach is underpinned by the ability to quickly interpret market data and adjust strategies accordingly, creating campaigns that are always relevant and engaging. Utilizing performance indicators to evaluate these campaigns ensures continuous improvement, aligning efforts with business goals and maximizing return on investment.

An example of incorporating agility into a marketing strategy can be seen in real-time marketing efforts. These involve capitalizing on current events or trending topics to connect with audiences meaningfully and dynamically. Such a model demands readiness to pivot marketing efforts based on immediate feedback and the outcomes of each campaign phase. Employing tools such as Trello or JIRA can help organize and streamline processes, ensuring all stakeholders are aligned and able to move forward efficiently despite any internal or external changes.

While traditional marketing methods often relied on set calendars and long-term planning, the modern agile methodology prioritizes quick decision-making and iterative progress. Incremental delivery allows marketing teams to test portions of their campaigns early and make necessary adjustments before full-scale rollouts, reducing the risk of outdated or irrelevant messaging. This adaptability aligns with contemporary consumer expectations, which favor timely and responsive interactions over static, long-drawn-out campaigns.

10.4 Leveraging Emotional Connections in Branding

In today's competitive market, understanding how emotional connections enhance brand loyalty and effectiveness is crucial for entrepreneurs, marketers, and social media managers. Emotional storytelling is a key element in building these deep connections, as exemplified by Nike's campaigns. Nike skillfully utilizes narratives that go beyond promoting products to cultivating a sense of belonging and inspiration. By sharing stories of athletes overcoming adversity or striving for greatness, Nike fosters an emotional bond with its audience. These stories resonate on a personal level, leading consumers to identify with the brand values. As a result, Nike enjoys repeated consumer interactions and enduring loyalty.

Inclusive messaging also plays a vital role in expanding a brand's appeal and engagement. In a globalized world, audiences are diverse, and brands that embrace this diversity can significantly broaden their reach. By crafting messages that resonate with a wide range of demographics, brands invite more people into their community. Inclusion involves recognizing and celebrating differences, whether cultural, social, or lifestyle-based. Through thoughtful representation in advertising and content, brands create a welcoming atmosphere that appeals to various customer segments. This approach not only broadens brand appeal but also fosters a sense of belonging among customers, which enhances brand loyalty.

Consistency across channels is another essential component that strengthens brand values and enhances recognition. For brands to maintain a coherent identity, they need to deliver consistent messages regardless of where their audience encounters them. Whether through social media, advertisements, or packaging, uniformity in tone, style, and core values reinforces familiarity. When consumers recognize a brand consistently, it builds trust and reliability, making it easier for them to engage and remain loyal. Consistent messaging ensures that customers receive the same brand experience, no matter the platform, which leads to greater brand awareness and recall.

Moreover, rapid audience response and adaptability can greatly increase brand relatability and sales, as demonstrated by Old Spice. The brand saw immense success by quickly responding to current trends and engaging directly with its audience. Through witty and humorous content, delivered promptly and tailored to ongoing conversations, Old Spice managed to capture attention and create buzz. This agility allowed the brand to stay relevant and relatable, encouraging consumers to interact with their content and purchase their products. By being adaptable and responsive, brands can seize opportunities to connect with their audience, ultimately boosting sales and strengthening their market position.

To effectively create emotional engagement in marketing, several strategies can be employed. A customer-centric approach is foundational, where marketing messages are personalized to align with individual needs and preferences, demonstrating empathy and understanding. Authenticity is equally important; brands must stay true to themselves and communicate honestly, inspiring trust and fulfilling audience expectations. Social impact and inclusion efforts, highlighted through marketing, evoke emotions necessary for building meaningful connections, aligning initiatives with consumer values. Emotionally-charged content, through stories, anecdotes, or humor, elicits reactions that leave lasting impressions, while maintaining a consistent brand voice helps establish familiarity across all touchpoints. Embracing negative emotions strategically can also contribute to engagement, although it requires careful execution to avoid long-term negative impacts.

Measuring and evaluating emotional engagement is crucial for understanding its effectiveness. Primary research, such as customer surveys and interviews, provides insights into emotional responses and satisfaction levels. Sentiment analysis, through social listening, further captures consumer emotions in real-time, revealing valuable information about consumer perceptions and reactions to branding efforts. Brands that rig-orously analyze these metrics can fine-tune their strategies to better meet emotional needs and improve overall engagement.

Emotional marketing delivers significant benefits— from en-hanced brand loyalty to improved profitability. When brands successfully tap into emotional connections, they not only differentiate themselves in the marketplace but also foster strong relationships with their consumers. Thus, leveraging emotional engagement becomes a powerful tool for any brand looking to grow its presence and ensure long-term success in today's dynamic marketing landscape.

10.5 The Role of Community Engagement in Marketing Success

In the ever-evolving landscape of social media marketing, community engagement is a vital strategy that can signif-icantly enhance the effectiveness of marketing campaigns. By fostering genuine connections with audiences, brands can build trust, authenticity, and loyalty, ultimately driving successful outcomes. One of the most compelling examples of community engagement is user-generated content (UGC), notably utilized by Airbnb. This approach leverages stories and experiences shared by real users, which not only resonates with potential customers but also builds a sense of community around the brand. When individuals see authentic narratives from their peers, it instills confidence and trust in the brand, making them more likely to engage and convert. This strategy underscores the power of UGC as a tool for creating a relatable and trustworthy brand image.

Personalized marketing is another powerful aspect of effective community engagement, exemplified by Coca-Cola's "Share a Coke" campaign. By replacing their iconic logo with popular names on bottles, Coca-Cola invited consumers to find their name and share their experiences online. This personalized touch sparked widespread participation and sharing, significantly amplifying the campaign's reach and impact. It demonstrated the potential of personal connections in marketing—consumers became active participants and ambassadors of the brand, spreading its message organically across social networks. The key takeaway here is that personalization fosters deeper connections with consumers, leading to increased interaction and brand visibility.

However, community engagement must be carefully managed to avoid unintended consequences, as illustrated by McDonald's #McDStories campaign. Initially launched to share heartwarming customer stories, it quickly backfired as users began posting negative experiences. This incident highlights the importance of having robust moderation and crisis management strategies in place when engaging the community, especially on open platforms like social media. Managing these interactions effectively requires anticipating potential risks and preparing to address issues promptly and transparently. By doing so, brands can mitigate damage and maintain a positive reputation while still benefiting from community contributions.

A crucial aspect of maintaining brand integrity during crises is swift, empathetic communication, a lesson learned from United Airlines. In situations where public perception can turn rapidly, clear and compassionate responses are essential to preventing long-lasting tarnish to a brand's image. Following a widely publicized incident involving passenger treatment, United Airlines faced massive backlash, exacerbated by their delayed and insufficient initial response. Effective crisis management requires addressing concerns immediately and sincerely to rebuild trust with both the affected parties and the broader audience. This emphasizes the need for preparedness and agility in communication strategies, ensuring that the brand's values and empathy are consistently conveyed during challenging times.

Community engagement goes beyond crisis management; it's about building lasting relationships with audiences. Consistent interaction and attention to feedback through social listening allow brands to adapt and evolve in response to their community's needs and preferences. Engaged communities provide valuable insights into consumer behavior, enabling brands to refine their marketing strategies continually. Listening to what customers say about your brand can guide strategic decisions and drive innovation, ensuring that marketing efforts remain relevant and impactful over time.

Authentic conversations are integral to fostering community engagement. Gone are the days of one-way marketing messages that talk at consumers rather than with them. Today's brands succeed by embracing two-way dialogues, where they actively participate in conversations with their audience. Responding to comments, questions, and messages not only humanizes the brand but also strengthens the emotional connection with consumers. It's an opportunity to showcase the brand's culture and values, thereby enhancing trust and credibility. Authenticity in conversations helps build a loyal following that sees the brand as more than just a transactional entity, but as a valued part of their life experience.

Word-of-mouth marketing, driven by satisfied customers who become advocates for the brand, is a testament to the success of community engagement. When customers have positive experiences, they naturally share them, often without any prompting or compensation. This organic advocacy is potent, as recommendations from peers hold significant weight in purchasing decisions. Brands that successfully engage their community create environments where happy customers willingly spread the word, further solidifying brand reputation and expanding reach.

10.6 Final Thoughts

In this chapter, we explored successful brand campaigns and their strategies, providing valuable insights for entrepreneurs, marketing professionals, and social media managers. Campaigns like Nike's "Just Do It" and Coca-Cola's "Share a Coke" demonstrated the power of emotional and personalized connections in engaging audiences effectively. Likewise, Airbnb and Old Spice showed how humor and user-generated content can foster authenticity and relatability. These case studies serve as benchmarks, highlighting key elements such as audience understanding and personal resonance in crafting impactful campaigns.

Drawing lessons from both successes and failures is crucial for any business aiming to enhance its social media presence. By analyzing what worked well, brands can adopt strategies that align with their audience's values and emotions, thus building stronger relationships and increasing loyalty. Understanding past pitfalls, such as those experienced by Pepsi or McDonald's, further informs robust crisis management and audience engagement tactics. As the digital landscape continues to shift, applying these insights will help businesses remain agile, ensuring their efforts resonate and lead to desired outcomes.

Chapter 11: Overcoming Common Challenges

O vercoming common challenges in social media marketing involves tackling obstacles that frequently arise in the field. This landscape, filled with rapid shifts and public scrutiny, presents unique hurdles for those tasked with managing an online presence. Missteps can lead to crises, while relentless engagement demands can contribute to burnout among managers. However, these challenges also offer opportunities for growth and learning, paving the way for stronger brand connections and more effective communication strategies.

In this chapter, readers will gain insights into three key areas of focus: handling negative feedback, managing social media crises, and preventing burnout. Each section provides practical advice tailored for entrepreneurs, small business owners, marketing professionals, and social media managers. Readers will learn how to transform negative feedback into valuable insights, enabling their brands to adapt and improve. They will explore methods for identifying and navigating social media crises with poise and precision, ensuring minimal disruption to brand reputation. Finally, strategies to maintain a healthy work-life balance while fostering a creative environment are discussed, addressing the critical issue of burnout. Through these explorations, the chapter equips readers with the tools needed to thrive in the dynamic world of social media marketing.

11.1 Dealing with Negative Feedback

In the realm of social media marketing, negative feedback is inevitable. However, instead of viewing it as a setback, marketers and entrepreneurs should see it as an invaluable tool for gaining insights and driving improvement. Negative feedback can serve as a mirror that reflects the perceptions and expectations of your audience, offering candid snapshots of areas where your products or services may fall short. According to Tasha Eurich, negative feedback allows us to monitor performance and alert us to significant changes needed. When approached strategically, this feedback becomes a roadmap that guides your business towards enhanced customer satisfaction and loyalty.

To harness the potential of negative feedback effectively, establishing a robust response protocol is essential. Speed and appropriateness are key. A timely response demonstrates that you value your customers' opinions and are committed to addressing their concerns. A structured approach to handling these situations not only mitigates potential damage but also turns critics into advocates. This involves having predefined guidelines on how to tackle various types of negative comments, ensuring that each response maintains professionalism and empathy.

Constructive engagement is another crucial facet of managing negative feedback. It's about creating a dialogue with your audience rather than a monologue. Encouraging open communication fosters trust and increases transparency, which in turn builds stronger relationships. Acknowledge the feedback publicly when appropriate, express gratitude for the insight shared, and invite further discussion if necessary. This approach shows that you are genuinely interested in improving and are committed to listening to your customers.

Moreover, criticism should be a learning opportunity, acting as a catalyst for enhancing your products and services. By dissecting negative feedback, businesses can identify common issues and implement necessary changes. Adapting based on customer feedback not only improves the quality of what you offer but also aligns your offerings more closely with market needs, increasing competitiveness. As noted by LinkedIn Learning, professional responses to feedback show emotional intelligence and maturity, enhancing reputation and relationships. This proactive stance not only helps in retaining existing customers but also attracts new ones through positive word-of-mouth and improved offerings.

When dealing with negative feedback, strategies to extract actionable insights become pivotal. Here, one might employ techniques such as categorizing feedback to identify patterns and recurring themes. In doing so, it is possible to address systemic issues rather than isolated incidents, making improvements more comprehensive and impactful. Using tools like surveys or direct follow-ups can help in gathering additional data, providing a clearer picture of the underlying problems.

Furthermore, involve your team in the feedback process. Encouraging employees to engage with customer feedback empowers them to contribute ideas for improvements, fostering a culture of continuous learning and innovation. It is important that everyone in the organization understands the value of feedback and feels invested in turning criticisms into better customer experiences.

Creating an environment where feedback is welcomed and acted upon requires consistency. Regular reviews and updates to your feedback management strategy ensure that it remains relevant and effective. By continuously refining these processes, businesses can stay agile and responsive to changing customer expectations and market dynamics.

11.2 Managing Social Media Crises

In today's fast-paced digital landscape, social media crises can arise swiftly and unexpectedly. For entrepreneurs, marketers, and social media managers, being equipped with the right tools to handle these situations is crucial. This guide provides a strategic approach to managing and mitigating social media crises effectively, ensuring minimal impact on your brand's reputation and public trust.

To begin with, early identification of potential crises through vigilant monitoring and sentiment analysis is a proactive step that cannot be overlooked. Social media platforms are vibrant ecosystems where discussions about brands occur continually.

By deploying robust monitoring tools like Brand24, businesses can track mentions and conversations in real time, allowing them to detect shifts in sentiment or unusual spikes in negative feedback. These tools not only monitor chatter but also perform sentiment analysis, providing insights into how audiences are engaging with your brand. Early detection by using monitoring tools serves as the first line of defense in preparing an appropriate response strategy.

Developing a crisis communication strategy is paramount in addressing issues quickly and consistently. A well-crafted plan involves devising standardized response templates to ensure uniformity in communication while tailoring messages for specific situations. Establishing a clear response protocol is crucial here. This should include choosing a spokesperson who is well-informed about the crisis to deliver consistent and reliable information, thus becoming the face of the brand during turbulent times. Regular updates keep followers informed and quell rumors, maintaining transparency and control over the narrative.

Once the immediate crisis has been addressed, conducting a rigorous post-crisis evaluation is essential to assess the impact and refine future strategies. This process involves a comprehensive review of actions taken, engagement levels, and overall outcomes. Gathering insights from various teams provides a holistic understanding of the crisis management performance. Debriefing sessions should identify strengths and areas for improvement, ensuring that lessons learned are incorporated into updated protocols. Such evaluations foster organizational resilience, making the team better prepared for any future challenges.

Throughout the crisis and its aftermath, maintaining public trust is imperative. Transparent communication practices, coupled with timely solutions, show empathy and reliability. Acknowledge the situation openly and offer concrete steps towards resolution. Engaging directly with consumers, addressing their concerns, and focusing on constructive dialogue can help rebuild any lost trust. It's vital to create a two-way communication channel with your audience, fostering a sense of connection and commitment in resolving issues.

Furthermore, utilizing the viral nature of social media to mobilize support and disseminate accurate information can help amplify your efforts in turning the crisis around. Encouraging positive interactions and leveraging the power of collective action can shift focus away from the negative aspects of the crisis. This approach not only reinforces your brand's values but also portrays your organization as a proactive entity dedicated to customer satisfaction.

11.3 Preventing Burnout in Social Media Management

Burnout is a significant concern for social media managers, who often find themselves constantly connected and responsible for creating engaging content under tight deadlines. Recognizing the early signs of burnout is critical to addressing this issue effectively. Common indicators include heightened irritability, fatigue, reduced performance, and disengagement from work. Physical symptoms may manifest as headaches or sleep disturbances, while mental signs can include concentration difficulties and feelings of helplessness. It's essential for social media managers to be aware of these indicators in both themselves and their team members to take timely action.

To prevent burnout, implementing personal boundaries between work and personal life is crucial. Social media never sleeps, but humans require downtime to recharge. Managers should establish specific hours dedicated to work-related tasks and unplug from social media outside these hours. Utilizing scheduling tools can help maintain a consistent online presence without requiring constant manual input. Setting aside time each day to disconnect from technology promotes a healthier balance and allows individuals to focus on other aspects of life, fostering overall well-being.

Collaborating with colleagues and seeking support is another effective strategy to combat burnout. Sharing responsibilities prevents any single individual from bearing the entire burden. Encouraging open communication about workloads and challenges can foster a supportive work environment. Within teams, it's vital to create a culture where asking for help is not seen as a weakness but as an opportunity to enhance productivity and creativity. Support groups, both within and outside of work, offer invaluable emotional support and practical solutions, enhancing resilience against stress and pressure.

Professional development plays a significant role in maintaining enthusiasm and passion for social media management. Regular training and learning opportunities keep skills sharp and allow managers to stay updated with the latest trends and tools. Taking courses or attending workshops can reignite interest in the field and introduce fresh ideas for content strategies. Furthermore, setting personal career goals provides motivation and direction, ensuring that daily tasks align with long-term aspirations. Employers can support this by providing resources for professional growth, leading to increased job satisfaction and reduced burnout risk.

Incorporating wellness practices into daily routines can further mitigate burnout risk. Simple activities such as meditation, yoga, or even short walks can significantly enhance mental health. Encouraging breaks during work hours helps prevent exhaustion and keeps energy levels high throughout the day. Social media managers should also monitor their physical health, prioritizing regular exercise, balanced nutrition, and sufficient sleep. These practices contribute to greater resilience against stress and improve overall quality of life.

Creating an environment that promotes work-life balance is equally important. Flexible work arrangements, such as remote work options, empower social media managers to tailor their schedules according to personal needs, reducing the feeling of being overwhelmed. Encouraging use of annual leave and discouraging the habit of working through vacations are policies that highlight the importance of rest and recuperation. By valuing employees' time off, companies show commitment to their team's well-being, which can boost morale and productivity.

Furthermore, managing workload effectively is key to preventing burnout. Regular audits of social media strategies can identify redundant or low-impact tasks, allowing managers to focus on high-value activities. Streamlining processes and utilizing automation tools for routine tasks can alleviate pressure, enabling managers to concentrate on creative and strategic planning. Establishing clear priorities ensures that efforts are directed towards achieving tangible results, reducing unnecessary stress.

Recognition and appreciation within the workplace are vital components of an anti-burnout strategy. Acknowledging and rewarding hard work fosters a positive atmosphere and motivates employees to continue performing at their best. Simple gestures like public recognition, bonuses, or professional development opportunities can have a profound impact on team morale. Implementing peer support systems further enhances this effect, as employees can share advice and experiences, offering mutual encouragement and understanding.

In conclusion, addressing burnout among social media managers requires a multifaceted approach. By recognizing early signs, setting personal boundaries, fostering collaboration, prioritizing professional development, and promoting wellness, individuals and organizations can effectively mitigate burnout risks. A supportive work environment that values balance and recognizes achievements leads to happier, healthier employees who are more engaged and productive in their roles. Implementing these strategies not only benefits individual managers but also contributes to the overall success and sustainability of social media marketing efforts.

11.4 Establishing Effective Communication Protocols

Developing clear communication protocols is essential for social media marketers looking to navigate conflicts smoothly. Communication plays a critical role in conflict resolution, and building effective strategies can help businesses maintain their brand integrity while fostering positive interactions with their audience.

The first step in this process is understanding the importance of maintaining brand voice consistency across all communications. A consistent brand voice helps establish trust with your audience by ensuring that messages are cohesive and aligned with the company's values and identity, regardless of the platform or situation. Consistency isn't just about using the same language or tone; it also involves conveying messages that reflect the core principles of your brand. Whether responding to customer inquiries, managing feedback, or handling crises, sticking to a unified voice can make responses feel more authentic and reassuring to your audience.

In addition to consistency, balancing empathy and professionalism in public interactions is crucial. Social media offers a direct line to your customers, who often seek immediate and empathetic responses. Demonstrating empathy involves acknowledging the customer's feelings and showing genuine concern for their experience or issue. However, it is equally important to maintain professionalism. This means addressing concerns with a composed demeanor and offering practical solutions without letting emotions dictate the interaction. A professional yet empathetic approach can prevent misunderstandings and create a more positive perception of your brand.

Creating standardized templates tailored for timely and effective responses allows teams to handle situations efficiently while maintaining the brand's integrity. Templates can be pre-approved messages for common scenarios, such as inquiries, complaints, or compliments, enabling quick reactions without compromising quality. These templates should include guidelines for personalization to avoid sounding robotic and ensure that responses remain sincere. By having these templates at hand, team members can focus more on the specificities of each case rather than crafting new messages from scratch every time.

Another component of smooth conflict navigation is the importance of regular team meetings. These meetings ensure alignment and readiness for potential issues and provide a forum for discussing ongoing challenges and sharing updates on current protocols. Regular interaction among team members helps reinforce strategies, allowing everyone to stay informed about recent changes or enhancements within the brand's communication plan. Scheduling frequent meetings encourages continuous learning, fosters collaboration, and ensures that everyone feels confident and equipped to handle any situation that arises.

Furthermore, it is beneficial to create an open environment where team members are encouraged to share learnings with the group. Analyzing past conflicts together can shed light on effective approaches and areas of improvement. By openly discussing what worked and what didn't, teams can refine their strategies and become better prepared for future challenges. This collaborative process not only strengthens individual capabilities but also enhances the team's overall effectiveness in dealing with conflicts.

For example, imagine a scenario where a negative review about a product goes viral on social media. Having clear communication protocols in place enables the team to respond swiftly with consistent messaging that reflects both the brand's values and professionalism. A standardized template can serve as a useful guide for the team member responsible for addressing the complaint, ensuring they offer a suitable apology, propose a solution, and express gratitude for the customer's feedback— all within the framework of the company's voice.

11.5 Promoting Positive Engagement and Brand Loyalty

In today's digital landscape, fostering positive engagement is paramount for building loyal communities online. Social media marketers often face the challenge of managing interactions in a way that not only addresses concerns but also strengthens relationships with their audience. An effective approach involves turning negative experiences into opportunities to showcase exceptional service.

Imagine a scenario where a customer posts a critical comment on your social media page. Rather than viewing this as a mere complaint, consider it an opportunity to demonstrate dedication to customer care. Responding with empathy and offering a prompt, thoughtful solution can transform a dissatisfied customer into a brand advocate. This strategy not only resolves the immediate issue but also sets a standard for your community, showing others that you value transparency and customer-centric responses. By addressing complaints with genuine concern and action, your brand can turn critics into champions, reinforcing trust within your community.

Encouraging direct interaction and follow-up with your audience plays a crucial role in solidifying connections. Initiating conversations beyond initial transactions shows audiences they are valued beyond purchases. Personalized follow-ups—such as thank-you messages or check-ins after a service experience—enhance the perception of care and attentiveness. These interactions are not only appreciated but often lead to increased loyalty and advocacy. Members who feel personally connected to a brand are more likely to engage consistently and participate actively within the community. Regular communication, tailored to individual preferences and past interactions, deepens relationships and fosters a sense of belonging, thereby nurturing a more robust online community.

Documenting feedback trends is another essential practice for continuous improvement in brand messaging. Regular analysis of comments, suggestions, and inquiries can offer insights into what resonates with your audience. By identifying patterns and common themes, you gain valuable information to refine your communication strategies. This ongoing process ensures that your brand messaging remains relevant and aligned with audience expectations. For instance, noticing frequent requests for a particular feature can guide product development efforts, demonstrating that you listen to and act upon feedback. As you adapt your messaging based on documented feedback, your community will realize their voices contribute to shaping the brand, further encouraging participation and loyalty.

Creative campaigns serve as powerful tools for engaging audiences and reinforcing brand values. Consider designing initiatives that resonate with your community's interests and aspirations. Such campaigns can take the form of interactive challenges, storytelling contests, or cause-driven endeavors that align with your brand ethos. Engaging content captivates participants, making them eager to share experiences and spread the word about your brand. For example, a challenge encouraging users to showcase creative uses of your product can highlight its versatility while generating user-generated content, amplifying your brand message organically. Creative campaigns not only engage but also imbue your community with shared values, strengthening the communal bond over time.

To illustrate, let's explore a hypothetical campaign by a sustainable fashion brand that encourages customers to repurpose old garments into new fashion pieces. By promoting sustainability—a core brand value—the campaign engages consumers creatively while advocating for environmental consciousness. Participants sharing their projects across social media platforms weave these values into larger discussions, promoting both individual creativity and brand principles. As the campaign unfolds, the brand solidifies its place in the community as a leader in eco-friendly innovation.

11.6 Final Thoughts

In this chapter, we explored the challenges that social media marketers face, focusing on effectively handling negative feedback, managing crises, and preventing burnout. We delved into strategies for transforming negative interactions into opportunities for improvement by using feedback constructively. By establishing protocols for quick, empathetic responses and encouraging open dialogue, businesses can convert dissatisfied customers into loyal advocates. Additionally, recognizing signs of burnout and implementing wellness practices are essential for maintaining personal well-being and ensuring sustained productivity in a demanding digital environment.

Social media marketers must also be equipped to manage potential crises with proactive measures, like sentiment analysis and clear communication plans. By doing so, they protect their brand's reputation and maintain public trust. Empowering teams through robust monitoring tools and collaborative practices fosters an agile response to challenges, while prioritizing personal and professional development helps prevent exhaustion. Ultimately, these approaches allow marketers to build resilient communities and maintain positive engagement, driving brand loyalty and success in the evolving landscape of social media.

Chapter 12: Resources for Continuous Learning

C ontinuous learning in social media marketing is a matter of staying equipped with the right resources and tools to ensure lasting success beyond the initial stages. As the digital landscape evolves, it becomes crucial for professionals to not only keep pace but also strategically harness these changes for their benefit.   In this context, understanding which industry tools can streamline operations or enhance productivity can make a substantial difference in achieving marketing objectives. Moreover, building a habit of seeking credible information sources helps filter through the noise and focus on insights that drive real results. Whether it's engaging with thought leaders through newsletters or exploring new strategies via podcasts, each effort contributes significantly to maintaining relevance in an ever-changing environment.

This chapter thoroughly examines the resources available for nurturing long-term success in social media endeavors. First, it delves into industry-leading tools and platforms, explaining how they can optimize account management and analytics tracking, thus saving time and improving efficiency. Then, it highlights the value of subscribing to credible newsletters and podcasts, offering regular updates and expert insights. Following this, the chapter emphasizes the importance of community engagement, showcasing ways to tap into collective knowledge through forums and networks. Lastly, it explores educational resources and the continuous honing of skills through courses, webinars, and certifications. Collectively, these elements form a comprehensive framework for anyone looking to excel in social media marketing today and tomorrow.

12.1 Accessing Industry-Leading Tools and Platforms

In the dynamic world of social media marketing, efficiently managing multiple accounts is crucial for businesses aiming to maintain a consistent online presence. Social media management tools have become indispensable in this regard, offering features that streamline scheduled posts and automate analytics tracking. By utilizing these tools, entrepreneurs and marketing professionals can significantly reduce the time spent on manual updates across different platforms. For small business owners, these tools ensure that messages reach their audience at optimal times without constant monitoring.

One of the primary benefits of social media management tools is their ability to schedule posts ahead of time. Consistency is key in maintaining engagement with an audience, and a well-planned content calendar helps achieve that. These tools allow users to create a batch of posts, assigning specific times and dates for publishing across various channels. This automatic scheduling not only saves time but also ensures that followers receive regular updates, even during off-hours or holidays.

With streamlined processes, businesses can focus more on crafting quality content rather than worrying about its timely delivery.

Moreover, automating analytics tracking offers quick insights into how posts perform. Instead of manually collecting data from each platform, these tools provide consolidated reports showing metrics such as likes, shares, comments, and click-through rates. This real-time feedback allows businesses to adapt their strategies promptly, ensuring content remains relevant and engaging. Automated analytics tracking thus facilitates faster decision-making and enhances the overall efficiency of marketing campaigns.

Facilitating team collaboration is another significant advantage of using these tools. Many social media management systems offer features that support teamwork, enabling multiple users to contribute to a single campaign seamlessly. With centralized dashboards, team members can track progress, draft posts, and review one another's work without confusion. This collaborative environment fosters creativity and ensures consistency across all outputs, which is particularly beneficial for marketing agencies and teams working on large-scale projects.

Beyond management, analytics platforms play a pivotal role in understanding audience behavior and refining marketing efforts. These platforms dive deep into user engagement, helping businesses identify content that truly resonates with their target demographics. Understanding what drives interactions—be it certain topics, visuals, or posting times—

allows marketers to tailor their strategies accordingly. Moreover, analytics tools measure critical conversion metrics, such as sales generated from social media referrals. This data-driven approach enhances the precision of marketing tactics, ultimately leading to improved ROI and sustained growth.

The importance of content creation tools cannot be overstated in the realm of social media marketing. These tools are designed to simplify the content generation process by providing templates and advanced editing capabilities for both written and visual materials. Templates serve as starting points that maintain brand aesthetics while reducing the time needed to craft individual posts. Meanwhile, advanced editing features enable users to fine-tune their content, ensuring it aligns perfectly with brand messaging. Importantly, many content creation tools now integrate directly with social media platforms, making the publication process seamless and efficient.

Ad management systems further complement these efforts by optimizing ad spending through data-driven strategies. These systems analyze vast amounts of data to pinpoint the most effective approaches for audience targeting and budget allocation. One powerful capability is A/B testing, where different versions of an ad campaign are tested simultaneously to determine which performs better. This iterative process allows marketers to refine their strategies continuously, maximizing the return on investment for each advertising dollar spent.

Effective audience targeting is another significant benefit provided by ad management systems. By utilizing user data, these systems can segment audiences based on interests, behaviors, and demographics, ensuring ads reach those most likely to engage with the content. This targeted approach reduces wasted resources on uninterested users and increases the chances of meaningful interaction and conversion. A personalized ad experience enhances consumer satisfaction, leading to higher loyalty and brand advocacy.

Guidelines for effectively using these tools include establishing clear objectives before selecting software, evaluating tool features against business needs, and training team members to leverage all functionalities. Additionally, regularly reviewing software effectiveness and staying updated with new features ensures the tools continue to meet changing business demands.

12.2 Subscribing to Credible Newsletters and Podcasts

In the ever-evolving landscape of social media marketing, staying informed is essential for long-term success. To maintain an edge in this dynamic field, it is crucial to follow thought leaders who are at the forefront of the industry. This approach not only keeps marketers updated on current trends and innovations but also provides actionable insights that enhance practical knowledge and skills.

Industry newsletters serve as an invaluable resource for professionals aiming to stay abreast of the latest developments. These newsletters compile insights from market experts, highlight emerging trends, and share innovative strategies designed for immediate application. The convenience and accessibility of these newsletters make it easy for busy entrepreneurs, marketing professionals, and social media managers to integrate new ideas into their existing tactics without significant time investment. Whether it's learning about a recent algorithm change or discovering a cutting-edge engagement strategy, newsletters provide a steady stream of relevant information.

Marketing podcasts are another effective tool for continuous learning. By offering interviews with industry leaders, in-depth case studies, and discussions on evolving marketing techniques, podcasts provide listeners with a wealth of knowledge that can be absorbed during commutes or daily routines. The conversational format allows listeners to hear directly from those who have navigated complex marketing challenges and achieved success. For instance, tuning in to episodes featuring successful campaigns gives listeners insight into real-world applications of marketing theories and principles. Notably, the narratives and strategies shared by seasoned marketers can inspire new approaches and encourage creative thinking.

Webinars and online courses offer interactive opportunities to engage directly with experts in the field. Unlike traditional learning methods, webinars often feature live Q&A sessions, allowing participants to clarify doubts and gain deeper understanding of specific topics. Beyond the live session, many webinars provide post-session resources such as slides and supplementary readings that reinforce learning objectives. Similarly, online courses often include forums for peer interaction, fostering a community of learners who can exchange ideas and solutions. These platforms equip learners with practical skills that translate directly into improved marketing practices, thus making them highly valuable for both beginners and seasoned professionals.

The influence of successful social media personalities cannot be overlooked in the pursuit of continuous learning. Influencers wield significant power in shaping consumer perceptions and behaviors, and analyzing their strategies can yield profound insights. Observing how influencers create content, engage with their audience, and leverage various platforms unveils tactical approaches that can be adapted and implemented across different business models. Furthermore, many influencers share behind-the-scenes content and strategic breakdowns, providing a transparent view of their methods. This transparency helps demystify the process of growing a brand on social media and offers practical lessons in authenticity, consistency, and community-building.

To maximize the benefits of following thought leaders, adopting a systematic approach is advisable. Begin by identifying key individuals whose expertise aligns with your interests and professional goals. Diversifying sources ensures exposure to a range of perspectives and methodologies. Subscribing to multiple newsletters, incorporating diverse podcasts into your weekly routine, and participating in specialized webinars will keep your knowledge base robust and multifaceted. Additionally, maintaining an open mindset and willingness to experiment with newfound tactics is vital to translating insights into tangible results.

12.3 Engaging with Community Forums and Networks

Engaging with professional communities in social media marketing is an essential strategy for individuals seeking to advance their knowledge and effectiveness. In a rapidly evolving industry, staying informed and connected can make a significant difference in career success and personal growth. These communities provide unique opportunities to learn, share, and collaborate with others who face similar challenges and triumphs.

One of the most accessible forms of community engagement is through online forums such as Reddit. Platforms like these offer excellent spaces for advice sharing and discovering innovative solutions. With participants from diverse backgrounds and levels of expertise, users can post questions, share insights, and explore new ideas. This dynamic exchange of information helps marketers stay updated on trends and best practices, fostering continuous learning. For example, a marketer struggling with algorithm changes might find effective strategies shared by peers who have faced the same challenges. The collaborative nature of these forums ultimately enhances problem-solving skills and encourages creative approaches to marketing challenges.

Social media groups also play a vital role in creating safe spaces for professionals to discuss industry-related issues and receive real-time feedback. These groups, often found on platforms such as Facebook or LinkedIn, bring together marketers to engage in discussions about campaign performance, tool selection, and strategic planning. By participating in these conversations, members gain immediate access to peer-driven advice and support. They can troubleshoot current problems, brainstorm potential solutions, and validate strategies through collective wisdom. For instance, a social media manager looking for ways to increase engagement might test out suggestions from group discussions and implement them to gauge effectiveness, leading to improved outcomes for their brand.

Beyond virtual interactions, networking events and meetups offer invaluable opportunities for face-to-face engagement. These gatherings facilitate connections between professionals who share interests and goals, thereby expanding networks and providing insights from shared experiences. Attending such events allows individuals to interact directly with industry thought leaders, participate in hands-on workshops, and attend educational sessions. The exchange of knowledge and experiences can inspire new ideas and strategies for tackling social media marketing challenges. Moreover, building personal relationships at these events often leads to future collaborations and partnerships that can have lasting impacts on professional growth and success.

Professional organizations serve as another crucial resource for engaging with communities in social media marketing. Joining these organizations connects members with mentorship opportunities and exclusive resources designed to foster growth and development. Many professional bodies offer training programs, seminars, and conferences tailored to the needs of marketing professionals. Through these venues, members not only gain access to cutting-edge tools and techniques but also receive guidance from experienced mentors. A mentor can provide personalized advice, help navigate career paths, and introduce mentees to influential contacts within the industry. As a result, membership in such organizations can significantly enhance one's skills, credibility, and confidence.

12.4 Leveraging Educational Resources for Skill Development

Continuous skill development is crucial for professionals striving to maintain a competitive edge in social media marketing. Structured educational resources are indispensable tools that not only provide foundational knowledge but also aid in adapting to the ever-evolving digital landscape. Let's explore how online courses, certifications, workshops, and e-books contribute significantly to this goal.

Online courses have become essential in the modern learning ecosystem, offering flexible and comprehensive lessons tailored to various aspects of social media marketing. These courses often encompass topics ranging from basic platform navigation to advanced strategies like data analytics and audience engagement techniques. For instance, many online courses include real-world applications where learners can apply theories in simulated environments, enhancing their understanding and retention. By offering insights from industry leaders and interactive content, these courses cater to diverse learning paces and preferences, making them ideal for entrepreneurs and marketing professionals alike.

Certifications from reputable programs serve as valuable assets in showcasing one's expertise and dedication to continuous learning. Obtaining a certification demonstrates a commitment to staying updated with the latest trends and technologies in social media marketing. Moreover, they provide a structured framework within which learners can develop niche skills. For example, specialized certifications in areas like content marketing or SEO can significantly enhance a professional's ability to devise effective digital strategies. By focusing on specific skills, these credentials not only elevate an individual's credibility but also open doors to advanced career opportunities. As the demand for skilled marketers rises, certifications become crucial in distinguishing oneself in a crowded job market.

Workshops offer hands-on experiences that are invaluable for mastering practical skills in an interactive environment. Unlike traditional classroom settings, workshops encourage active participation and peer-to-peer learning, fostering a collaborative atmosphere. Participants engage in activities such as campaign building, performance analysis, and creative brainstorming sessions, enabling them to gain practical insights into real-world scenarios. Additionally, workshops frequently feature seasoned marketers who share their experiences and provide guidance. This direct interaction allows attendees to learn from the successes and failures of others, refining their approaches accordingly. The opportunity to network with peers and experts further enriches the learning experience, making workshops an essential component of professional development.

E-books and guides provide another vital resource for continuous learning, allowing individuals to delve deeply into specific topics at their own pace. These materials offer in-depth analyses of various subjects, from emerging social media platforms to advanced engagement strategies. The flexibility of e-books means that readers can explore content in a non-linear fashion, focusing on areas most relevant to their needs. Authors often infuse their work with case studies, anecdotes, and expert interviews, providing rich, contextual learning experiences. E-books are particularly beneficial for those who prefer self-paced study or need to fit learning around busy schedules. They serve as both introductory and supplementary resources, accommodating varying levels of expertise and interest.

Incorporating these structured educational resources into one's professional development strategy fosters a well-rounded approach to learning. In an industry characterized by constant change, remaining informed and adaptable is paramount. Engaging with online courses, pursuing certifications, attending workshops, and studying e-books collectively empower individuals to navigate the dynamic world of social media marketing effectively. Each resource offers unique benefits: online courses for their structured curriculum, certifications for their credibility, workshops for their practical experience, and e-books for their depth of knowledge. Together, they form a comprehensive toolkit for anyone committed to achieving long-term success in digital marketing.

Moreover, embracing continuous education helps profession-als anticipate trends rather than merely react to them. By proactively expanding their skill sets, marketers can implement innovative strategies and leverage new technologies efficiently. This proactive stance not only enhances individual capabilities but also contributes to organizational growth and competitiveness. As marketing disciplines increasingly prioritize data-driven decision-making, the skills acquired through these educational resources enable practitioners to harness analytics, understand consumer behavior, and optimize campaigns with precision.

Furthermore, for entrepreneurs and small business owners, participating in these learning opportunities equips them with the necessary tools to build and sustain a strong brand presence. Understanding market dynamics and consumer interactions through learned methodologies ensures that their marketing efforts resonate with target audiences. It also empowers them to make informed decisions regarding platform selection, content creation, and audience engagement strategies, ultimately leading to increased sales and customer loyalty.

For marketing professionals and social media managers, these resources provide avenues to refine existing tactics and integrate new insights into their strategic planning. By staying current with industry developments and best practices, they can enhance campaign effectiveness and drive meaningful results for their organizations. The knowledge gained from these resources supports greater innovation and creativity in problem-solving, positioning them as valuable assets within their teams.

12.5 Monitoring Industry Trends and Innovations

In the dynamic and ever-evolving world of social media marketing, staying ahead of trends is vital for entrepreneurs, marketing professionals, and social media managers. The landscape can shift rapidly, driven by technological advances and changing consumer behaviors. Recognizing these shifts early on can equip a business with the insights needed to adjust strategies and maintain a competitive edge. One effective method is the regular review of industry reports, which provide comprehensive data on emerging trends and shifts in social media usage behaviors. These reports often compile information from surveys, market analyses, and expert opinions, offering invaluable foresights into what's next in the digital media sphere. A consistent analysis of such reports allows marketers to track changes over time, evaluate potential impacts on their brand strategies, and adapt accordingly to maintain relevance and engagement with their audience.

Attending conferences is another powerful avenue for staying informed about the latest innovations and discussions shaping the social media landscape. Conferences bring together industry leaders, innovators, and enthusiasts from around the globe, fostering an environment rich with learning opportunities. Participants gain exposure to cutting-edge technologies and novel approaches that could redefine how businesses engage with audiences online. For instance, discussions at recent conferences have highlighted increased reliance on artificial intelligence for content creation and customer interaction—an insight that savvy marketers can leverage to optimize their campaigns. Additionally, conferences offer networking opportunities, enabling attendees to connect with thought leaders and peers facing similar challenges, thereby broadening their professional perspectives and problem-solving toolkit.

Engaging with futurists and trend analysts offers an additional layer of foresight into the potential developments within marketing landscapes. These experts specialize in making informed predictions based on current data and historical patterns, providing a glimpse into future possibilities. By following their insights, marketers can remain proactive rather than reactive, preparing for upcoming challenges and opportunities before they fully materialize. This foresight is particularly important as emerging technologies like virtual reality and IoT continue to shape consumer expectations and social media functionalities. For example, the rise of augmented reality (AR) features in social media platforms has opened new avenues for immersive storytelling and user engagement, which trend analysts had predicted years earlier.

Adopting an experimental mindset is crucial in this fast-paced environment, encouraging marketers to test new strategies and tools before they become mainstream. An experimental approach involves being open to trial and error, embracing creative solutions, and continuously refining tactics based on results. This strategy enables businesses to identify and implement innovative practices that set them apart from competitors. Early adopters of groundbreaking technologies or techniques often enjoy first-mover advantages, capturing audience attention and loyalty through unique experiences. Experimentation also cultivates a culture of adaptability, empowering teams to pivot quickly when unforeseen changes

202

occur in the market.

Moreover, experimentation should be data-driven, where decisions are informed by analytics and performance metrics. Tracking key performance indicators (KPIs) allows marketers to assess the effectiveness of each initiative and make necessary adjustments to optimize outcomes. For instance, if a new AR campaign yields high levels of engagement, it suggests that the target audience finds value in interactive content, which can then inform future marketing efforts.

In addition to individual experimentation, collaborative experimentation can also foster innovation. Cross-functional teams comprising marketers, designers, technologists, and strategists can collaborate to brainstorm and test novel ideas. Such teamwork not only sparks creativity but also ensures a holistic approach that considers various aspects of the customer experience. Organizations that champion collaborative experimentation often see faster implementation of successful strategies due to shared insights and expertise.

To harness the full potential of these strategies, it's important to institutionalize continuous learning within organizations. Developing a learning culture that encourages curiosity, knowledge sharing, and skill enhancement can significantly contribute to sustained success in social media marketing. Employers might consider incentivizing attendance at industry events, promoting access to educational resources, or hosting internal workshops led by experts in the field.

SOCIAL MEDIA MARKETING SECRETS

12.6 Final Thoughts

The chapter highlighted essential tools and resources that are crucial for achieving long-term social media success. By utilizing industry-leading platforms, entrepreneurs and marketing professionals can efficiently manage multiple social media accounts and automate analytics tracking to maintain a consistent online presence. The value of subscribing to credible newsletters and podcasts, engaging with community forums, and leveraging educational resources was also emphasized as strategies that enhance one's understanding of current trends and best practices in social media marketing. These approaches allow professionals to stay informed, adapt swiftly to changes, and employ effective techniques to engage their audience consistently.

In addition to these tools and resources, the chapter underscored the importance of monitoring industry trends and innovations to remain competitive in an ever-evolving digital landscape. Attending conferences and engaging with trend analysts offer valuable insights into new technologies and strategies that marketers can leverage. Encouraging experimentation and fostering a culture of continuous learning within organizations further bolsters one's ability to implement innovative strategies. By combining these elements, entrepreneurs, small business owners, marketing professionals, and social media managers can build robust brand presences, executing well-informed plans that drive meaningful engagement and achieve sustained growth in the digital space.

Conclusion

As you reach the conclusion of this book, it's time to reflect on the journey you've undertaken and the insights you've gained. Social media marketing isn't just an aspect of modern business—it's a dynamic and integral part of creating and sustaining a brand presence that resonates with audiences. For entrepreneurs, small business owners, marketing professionals, and social media managers alike, mastering the art and science of social media is paramount.

Throughout this book, we have explored strategies designed to help you not only understand but effectively engage with your target audience across various social platforms. Consider the critical lessons shared: understanding platform demographics allows you to tailor your messages in a way that best suits the users you're trying to reach; crafting compelling content ensures that your message does more than just exist—it captivates and engages.

The landscape of social media is ever-evolving, and keeping pace requires both strategy and adaptability. Reflect on how each chapter has equipped you with foundational insights that serve as your roadmap, guiding you through the dynamic digital world. Whether it's utilizing analytics to refine your tactics or exploring new emerging platforms, these tools enable you to execute strategies with precision and creativity.

The time to put your knowledge into action is now. The theories and strategies discussed are only as powerful as the actions they inspire. Imagine sitting down today, envisioning the detailed plans for your next social media campaign. With a cup of coffee by your side and a clear vision fueled by the skills you've acquired, you're ready to draft your first comprehensive content plan. Your toolbox is filled with strategies just waiting to build your online presence and enhance your brand identity.

Remember, the true power of social media lies in its ability to forge connections—between individuals, between brands and consumers, and between ideas and innovation. Don't wait for the perfect moment; each day presents a new opportunity to create, connect, and grow. The strategies you've learned empower you to turn theory into practice, transforming abstract concepts into tangible results.

While these pages have armed you with essential skills, knowledge, and strategies, it's important to acknowledge that your journey doesn't end here. Social media marketing is not a one-time effort but an ongoing process of learning, adapting, and evolving. Just as trends shift and user behaviors change, so must your approaches and tactics.

Each post you craft, every campaign you launch, and all the interactions you cultivate are vital steps in a broader journey to establish and enhance your brand's presence. There will be challenges along the way, moments of uncertainty where strategies might need recalibration, but embrace these instances as opportunities for growth. A mindset of continuous learning and flexibility will keep your brand relevant and thriving amidst the ever-shifting tides of the digital world.

Moreover, cultivating a habit of staying informed and engaged with industry updates ensures you're never left behind. Dive into educational resources, attend webinars, and participate in social media forums to tap into a wealth of collective knowledge and experiences. Engaging with fellow marketers and community members opens windows to fresh perspectives, innovative ideas, and invaluable support systems. After all, while your journey is unique to you, it's bolstered by the shared experiences and insights of others navigating similar paths.

To sustain momentum and drive future growth, consider taking advantage of various resources that foster continued development and learning. Online communities and forums are rich sources of inspiration and guidance, allowing you to share experiences and gain insights from like-minded professionals. Dedicated platforms for social media marketing practitioners provide spaces to discuss recent trends, troubleshoot challenges, and celebrate successes.

Look toward influential blogs, podcasts, and newsletters for regular doses of expert commentary and emerging industry trends. These platforms can also serve as avenues to refine your strategies continuously and stay ahead of the curve. Investing time and energy into professional development pays dividends in the form of enhanced skills, deeper insights, and innovative solutions that set your brand apart.

In closing, whether you're an entrepreneur aiming to boost sales through strategic social media use or a marketing professional seeking to refine your expertise, know that you hold the key to unlocking immense potential within the social media realm. By applying the lessons learned and harnessing the tools provided, you're well-equipped to navigate the complexities of social media marketing with confidence and creativity.

Hold steadfast to the image of sitting at your workspace, penning the blueprint of an impactful social media campaign— each post, a brushstroke painting the portrait of your brand. Embrace the journey with determination and enthusiasm, knowing that each step forward strengthens your standing in the digital age.

This book has provided a foundation, but you are at the helm of your brand's narrative. Continuing to engage, learn, and innovate will ensure your place in the ever-changing world of social media marketing. Here's to the exciting road ahead and the remarkable possibilities that await your brand.

References

Expert Social Media Services to Drive Conversions | Dmezi. https://dmezi.com/services/social-media/

Everything You Need To Know About A B2B IT Marketing Agency. https://www.socialmediamagazine.org/b2b-it-marketing-agency/

What Is the Best Free Search Engine to Find Someone? - Tech Reviews Blog. https://english.amirinfobangla.com/what-is-the-best-free-search-engine-to-find-someone/

Where do leads come from? What you should know about lead sources! by LinkedCRM AI. https://linkedcrm.ai/pt/blog/where-do-leads-come-from-what-you-should-know-about-lead-sources

SHAFIYLA LYONI PUTRI (2024). EXPLORING LEARNING EXPERIENCE IN WATCHING LANGUAGE TEACHING PAGE ON INSTAGRAM AND TIKTOK FOR EFL STUDENT. https://core.ac.uk/download/621979320.pdf

ChatSonic Review 2023: AI-Powered Chatbot For Bloggers -

David Ruhm. https://www.davidruhm.com/ai/chatsonic-review/

Content Marketing and Copywriting - SkyFall Blue. https://www.skyfallblue.com/services/content-marketing-and-copywriting/

Montreal SEO: Tips to Boost Organic Visibility | 2023. https://www.codemastersinc.com/post/montreal-seo-landscape-2023-top-expert-tips-to-boost-visibility

How To Create A Powerful Landing Page To Enhance Your Brand Identity?. https://www.digitaltechnologyguide.com/how-to-create-a-powerful-landing-page-to-enhance-your-brand-identity/

The Imperative of AI Adoption in Marketing. https://www.winwithmcclatchy.com/blog/ai-integration-in-marketing

Crisis-Proofing: Business Resilience Strategies. https://www.mcdaccginc.com/post/crisis-proofing

Fueling Growth: MoversBoost's Dynamic Approach to Moving Company Success – NewzHit. https://newzhit.com/fueling-growth-moversboosts-dynamic-approach-to-moving-company-success/

Seven game-changing tips for digital marketing. https://www.officerssacademy.com/post/seven-game-changing-tips-for-digital-marketing

8 Social Media Marketing Mistakes Every Brand Makes. https://303.london/blog/8-social-media-marketing-mist akes/

Interactive Workshop Archives - Vision2Success. https://www .vision2success.co/insights/mec-category/interactive-works hop/

Influencer Marketing | Brighton Marketing Company. https://brighton-marketing.com/influencer-marketing/

10 Ways To Increase Website Traffic | Media Cannibal. https://mediacannibal.com/10-ways-to-increase-website-traffic-copy/

How does Instagram grow your business? - Businesstimemag. https://businesstimemag.com/how-does-instagram-grow-your-business/

Benefits of Joining the ONDC Network via GlobalLinker & Steps to Join. https://mastercard.globallinker.com/bizforum/artic le/benefits-of-joining-the-ondc-network-via-globallinker-and-steps-to-join/100043

The Impact of Social Media on Modern Marketing Strategies – One Day Business. https://oneday-business.com/the-impact-of-social-media-on-modern-marketing-strategies/

Understanding Your Audience for Better Content Creation - Spry. https://sprybrands.com/understanding-your-audience -for-better-content-creation/

Maximizing Success with Google Ads: Precision, Flexibility, and Data-Driven Marketing – Dealey Media International. https://dealeymediainternational.com/maximizing-success-with-google-ads-precision-flexibility-and-data-driven-marketing/

Jordan Kasteler | Social Media Today. https://www.socialmediatoday.com/users/jordankasteler/

The Impact of Targeted Advertising on Casino Success | UTC Graphic. https://utcgraphic.com/the-impact-of-targeted-advertising-on-casino-success/

Unleashing the Power of Geo-targeting in Social Media for Luxury Brand Marketers. https://www.researchtheaffluent.com/post/unleashing-the-power-of-geo-targeting-in-social-media-for-luxury-brand-marketers/

How do I ensure that my branding resonates with a specific target audience? - Trace Brand Building. https://www.tracebrandbuilding.com/faq/how-do-i-ensure-that-my-branding-resonates-with-a-specific-target-audience/

The role of user-generated content in YouTube SEO. https://www.ichhori.com/2023/03/the-role-of-user-generated-content-in.html

Media Events 101: A Quick Primer - Mutant Communications. https://mutant.com.sg/media-events-101-a-quick-primer/

Brand Storytelling: Engaging Audiences Through Compelling

Narratives. https://presencemarketing.asia/brand-storytelli
ng-engaging-audiences-through-compelling-narratives/

Some Unique Content Strategy Examples!. https://marketingl
ad.io/unique-content-strategy-examples/

brand awareness | SUPPORTSOLUTIONSPANAMA. https://sup
portsolutionspanama.com/tag/brand-awareness

How to Improve Your Brand Building Using Customer Journey
Mapping - EasyBA.co. https://easyba.co/blog/business-anal
ysis/sales-and-marketing-analysis/how-to-improve-your-
brand-building-using-customer-journey-mapping/

Social Media Marketing w/ Video in Worcester, Massachusetts.
https://ignitemarketing.io/social-media-marketing-w-vide
o-in-worcester-massachusetts/

Social Media Personas: Types, Examples and 10 Tips for 2024
| Sprinklr. https://www.sprinklr.com/blog/social-media-per
sonas/

What Is Relationship Marketing? Definition, Types, And
Importance - Imarkguru.com. https://imarkguru.com/import
ance-of-relationship-marketing/

The Importance of Content Marketing Automation - NY Times
US. https://nytimesus.com/the-importance-of-content-mar
keting-automation/

Paid Advertising: What You Need to Know. https://seowind.io/

docs/paid-advertising-what-you-need-to-know/

Ephemeral Content: Drive Immediate Action & FOMO. https://hivo.co/blog/ephemeral-content-marketing-creating-fomo-and-driving-immediate-action

The Social Media Revolution: Transforming Celebrity Culture and Entertainment - inforisticblog.com. https://www.inforisticblog.com/2023/11/the-social-media-revolution-transforming-celebrity-culture-and-entertainment.html

How to Convert Social Media Followers into Loyal Customers: A Step-by-Step Guide - Startup Urban. https://www.startupurban.com/how-to-convert-social-media-followers-into-loyal-customers-a-step-by-step-guide/

Top Marketing Strategy: The 4 L's Of Lead Generation – B2B Lead Generation Services – Grow Your Business with Duo Leads. https://duoleads.com/top-marketing-strategy-the-4-ls-of-lead-generation/

8 Lessons to take you from Ecommerce Marketing Novice to Ecommerce Marketing Pro. https://www.zoziconsulting.com/post/8-lessons-to-take-you-from-ecommerce-marketing-novice-to-ecommerce-marketing-pro

Dive into Digital Strategies for Effective Marketing Campaigns – Fajar DOC. https://fajardoc.com/dive-into-digital-strategies-for-effective-marketing-campaigns/

The Growing Popularity Of Video Marketing. https://cleverbus

iness.ie/growing-popularity-of-video-marketing/

The Impact of Social Media on Consumer Buying Habits. https://forelight.ai/en/blog/the-impact-of-social-media-on-consumer-buying-habits

Dataczar - 9 Ways to Create a Solid Brand Strategy. https://www.dataczar.com/58192/9-ways-to-create-a-solid-brand-strategy/index.html

Innovative Influencer Marketing: Revolutionizing Business Marketing - TGPC. https://tgpc-clients.com/innovative-influencer-marketing-revolutionizing-business-marketing.html

Creative Ways To Use Promotional Items For Marketing | Oahu - Pedersen and Associates LLC Hawaii. https://www.rpahawaii.com/creative-ways-to-use-promotional-items-for-marketing-oahu/

Macro, Micro and Nano Influencers... Oh My! | Elevate My Brand. https://www.elevatemybrand.com/blog/macro-micro-and-nano-influencers-oh-my

How Brands Should Use Celebrities for Endorsements. http://celebrityprojects.com/how-brands-should-use-celebrities-for-endorsements/

Enhancing Your Social Media Reach for Business Success - Loak-in Blog. https://blog.loak-in.com/2024/03/29/enhancing-your-social-media-reach-for-business-success/

Digital Marketing Course in Vellore - Digital Marketing Institute in Vellore | Joy Innovations. https://www.joyinnovations. net/courses/digital-marketing-course-in-vellore/

SEO Metrics and Kpis You Should Be Tracking - TangerineSEO. https://tangerineseo.co.uk/seo-metrics-and-kpis-you-should-be-tracking/

The Benefits of Visualization Software | Lifestylemission. https://lifestylemission.com/the-benefits-of-visualization-software/

Marketers! Social Media ROI Improving! - DMNews. https://www.dmnews.com/marketers-social-media-roi-improving/

Youtube HashTag Extractor - Explore Trends - Toolsregion. https://toolsregion.com/youtube-hashtag-extractor/

How do I get 5k followers in one week on Instagram?. https://ve ntweek.com/how-do-i-get-5k-followers-in-one-week-on-instagram/

edocr - How To Get More Likes On Instagram?. https://www.e docr.com/v/e2eg8kj9/FourArrows/how-to-get-more-likes-on-instagram

How to Create a Content Framework that Will 10x Your Growth. https://www.singlegrain.com/blog/lu/create-content/

The Role of Video in Content Marketing: Trends and Predictions. https://blog.embedvid.io/the-role-of-video-in-conte

nt-marketing-trends-and-predictions/

Do you Need a Guide on How to Manage Your Artistic Marketing?. https://www.kadirajenningsart.com/post/do-you-need-a-guide-on-how-to-manage-your-artistic-marketing

Email Marketing vs. Social Media | Forge Apollo Philadelphia. https://forgeapollo.com/blog/email-marketing-vs-social-media/

Understanding Your Audience: Targeting and Segmentation in Social Media Marketing | C&I Studios. http://c-istudios.com/understanding-your-audience-targeting-and-segmentation-in-social-media-marketing/

The Role of Content Analytics in Social Media Marketing – Homepages Online. https://www.homepagesonline.com/2023/06/the-role-of-content-analytics-in-social-media-marketing/

The Importance of A/B Testing Your ASO Strategy - AppVector ASO Blog. https://blog.appvector.io/the-importance-of-a-b-testing-your-aso-strategy/

Harness the Power of Facebook and Google Ads to Grow Your Business | Skill Success Blog. https://blog.skillsuccess.com/facebook-and-google-ads-to-grow-your-business/

Boosting Engagement Through Enhanced Customer Communication – Glad your here!. https://blog.zingacp.com/2024/05/28/enhanced-customer-communication/

Social media reach - Empower Your Conversations with AI. https://inbaix.com/social-media-reach/

Social Media Trends to Watch in 2024: Stay Ahead of the Curve. https://www.rowschild.com/post/social-media-trends-202 4

Enhancing User Experience: EV Charging Session Monitoring - Smart Climate 2030. https://www.reneerb.com/enhancing-user-experience-ev-charging-session-monitoring/

Understanding How A/B Testing Works - Lunar Sky Games. https://lunarskygames.com/understanding-how-a-b-testin g-works-2/

Drive Brand Success With Social Media Marketing Services. https://digitalstrategeist.com/social-media-marketing-serv ices/

Influencer Marketing: What You Need to Know – Azura. https://azuramagazine.com/articles/influencer-marketing-what-you-need-to-know

Analyzing the Latest Trends in Social Media Marketing. https://beliked.me/analyzing-the-latest-trends-in-social-media-marketing/

Social Media Tools You Need to Try in 2023 - HeyTony. https://heytony.ca/social-media-tools-you-need-to-try-in-2023/

Knowing Your Audience: The Key to Social Media Success -
Quantum Social | Social Engagement Made Simple. https://qu
antumsocial.io/power-of-knowing-your-audience/

SEO-Optimized Blog Post Generator - Wordkraft. https://wor
dkraft.ai/ai-writer/seo-optimized-blog-post-generator/

AI Marketing - Elevate Your Marketing with AI. https://www.i
deamktg.com/grow/ai-marketing/

How do you stay updated with the latest trends and technologies in digital media? - Stories of Influence in Communication
and Media. https://digitalanswers.info/2024/02/22/how-do-
you-stay-updated-with-the-latest-trends-and-technologi
es-in-digital-media/

User-Generated Content and Social Media. https://learn-fro
m-ai.com/course/future-social-media/unit/32da45c7-0058
-4751-9db5-3c2b60f2e424